Get Ahead by Going Abroad

A WOMAN'S GUIDE TO FAST-TRACK CAREER SUCCESS

C. PERRY YEATMAN and
STACIE NEVADOMSKI BERDAN

Jacket design by HDN Studio

ISBN: 978-0-9839439-2-1, paperback
ISBN: 978-0-06-134053-6, hard cover

This book is dedicated —

by

Stacie Nevadomski Berdan to her daughters,

Connie and Betty

and

by

C. Perry Yeatman to her daughter,

Kirsten

Acknowledgments

From the Authors

This book is written by women, for women, and in praise of women. We could not have written it had it not been for the heroic women who came before us. We would like to recognize and celebrate all those who had the courage to live and work abroad.

We could not have written this book without the contributions of many people, and we thank them all. At the top of this list are four of the sensational women profiled herein: Anna Catalano, Diane Gulyas, Jacqualyn Fouse, and Patricia Kranz. Their thoughtful insight, good humor, and significant contribution of time – hundreds of combined hours – made the book much richer in texture and quality. We are also grateful to all the women who contributed quotes and took our survey online. Their personal anecdotes and stories added the human touch necessary to create a fun and lively text as seen through the eyes of real women who'd been there, and it encouraged us to continue to believe in the power of our idea.

We owe much gratitude to Steve Einhorn, friend and colleague, whose expert advice and guidance ensured our idea was backed up by credible third-party research. We also thank Steve McGarry for his professional insight and thoughtful commentary on today's global citizen.

We are grateful to our friends who took the time to read the manuscript before final submission: Annica Johansson, Michael Jacob Nevadomski, Carolyn Tieger, and Rebecca Weiner; we appreciate their thoughtful and honest feedback.

Last but not least, much appreciation goes to our agent, Denise Marcil, our publisher, HarperCollins, and our editor, Toni Sciarra. They took a chance on two new authors, believing in us and helping us creatively mold our idea into the book you hold in your hands.

From Stacie

I owe infinite gratitude to my husband, Mike, a published writer and former high-school English teacher, for his enduring support, almost unending patience, and oh-so-honest editorial feedback throughout the writing process. I'm a much better writer today because of his loving attention.

I appreciate my two wonderful daughters, Connie and Betty, who at the tender age of six grasped the importance of my writing this book – many times at the expense of weekends and excursions without me – and supported me with their warm hugs and fan club letters. They are future women of the world, and I wrote this book with them in mind.

Loving thanks go to my Mom, Constance Nevadomski, who has respected my individuality for as long as I can remember, and in memory of my father, Andrew Nevadomski, who inspired in me a love of travel and adventure. To my brothers and sisters – Nadine, Laura, Michael, Amy, Matthew, Ellen, and the spirit of my brother, A.J. – with whom I shared many fun-filled domestic and international adventures; being one of eight children certainly prepared me for navigating the complexities of corporate life.

I must give thanks to my mentors and colleagues at Burson-Marsteller, who provided an intense training ground and fulfilling professional home for 12 years. I will always be grateful to Carolyn Tieger and Bill Johnston, who took the time to mentor me in the early stages of my career and who encouraged me to move abroad. Heartfelt thanks also go to my Hong Kong colleagues whose friendship made my years in Hong Kong so much richer and rewarding.

From Perry

I must give my thanks first to those who have supported me in my journey from the beginning – my parents, Sandy and Penn Yeatman, and my siblings, Heather and P.J. I never would've had the nerve to leave the United States if I hadn't known they would be back at home, sending their love and being ready to support me, however needed.

I have also been blessed by a wonderful extended family. I thank my grandmothers, Dorothy Yeatman and Grace Perry, for being ahead of their time and showing me it was ok for a woman to be strong, opinionated, and self-sufficient. I'd also like to thank my aunts and uncles who were always so supportive and generous. I'm glad my wanderlust enabled us to spend so many great times together.

As for friends, despite my ever changing address, or perhaps because of it, I've gotten to know some of the most fabulous men and women in the world. I consider myself lucky to be able to call them my friends.

More recently, I've been blessed to have my own family. To my husband, Christian, I will forever be grateful fate saw fit to put our traveling souls in the same town at the same time. I couldn't have found a better partner for life's most amazing adventure – parenthood. To Kirsten and André, I could never fully express the joy and wonder they have added to my life so I will simply thank them for just being exactly who they are.

Finally, to all my bosses, colleagues, and clients, I will always be grateful for the lessons they taught me, the patience they showed me, the trust they put in me, and the opportunities they gave me – especially my current employer, Kraft Foods.

Contents

Chapter 1

Fast-tracking Your Career

I was a 25-year-old account executive making $25,000 a year when I accepted my first job overseas. By the time I returned to the United States 10 years later, I was a vice president in one of the world's largest consumer products companies, making more than 20-fold what I had when I left. More importantly, those years were the most exciting of my life, both personally and professionally: consulting for several of the world's most respected companies...having an office off Red Square while working on behalf of the Russian ministry of privatization... touring Bangkok with Margaret Thatcher. Weekends spent scuba diving in the Maldives, romantically strolling hand-in-hand through the streets of Prague and Paris, or shopping in the Grand Bazaar in Istanbul. I worked hard, played hard, learned a lot, and had fun. None of it would've happened if I'd stayed in the U.S.

— Perry, coauthor and Kraft Foods, Inc.

Going overseas can fast-track your career and expand your personal horizons beyond your wildest dreams. If you love adventure, thrive on taking risks and operating outside your comfort zone, and are fed up with the inequality of the old boys network, going global could be your ticket to the fast track.

As thousands of women (and men) know, working and living in another country can expand your professional options manifold. International experience differentiates you from your peers. Doors open for you because companies need professionals who can act locally while thinking globally.

Women in the know are onto this trend. More and more women are being asked to take on international dimensions in their existing jobs or are considering new jobs with more global dimensions – often at much earlier stages in careers than in the past. International roles, once offered primarily to men, are now increasingly being offered to women. There are many reasons, but the most groundbreaking is the growing acceptance that a woman's natural style – her feminine traits – can actually lead to greater success in cross-cultural situations. A woman's style endows her with an awareness of and ability to adapt to others' styles. It enables her to build teams in a non-threatening "we're all in this together" fashion. As women, we tend to over-communicate, which can actually be good in situations that are ambiguous and with people who are different from us. We persist diplomatically in difficult circumstances and are not afraid to use the right mix of emotional intelligence, intellectual might, and feminine intuition.

Companies are acknowledging this new fact of business by sending more women abroad than ever before. Don't misunderstand us; those gender stereotypes that have limited a woman's ability to be considered for an overseas assignment still exist. But they are slowly but surely diminishing as more women succeed in international assignments from Bangkok to Buenos Aires, Sao Paolo to Stockholm, Calcutta to Cairo. If you are looking for a ticket out of middle management, join our new band of leaders: women we call the new globetrotters because of the successful, international experiences they have under their belts (and in their pocketbooks).

Making It Real: Let the Adventure Begin

Throughout this book, you'll meet dozens of women who have catapulted their careers by going overseas. We surveyed more than 200 women who have spent significant time overseas, either as expatriates or in HQ-based roles with significant international responsibility. We designed the survey in consultation with a seasoned research expert. Invitations to participate were sent to approximately 100 female professionals who have worked overseas and then to hundreds more as referrals from those women to others they know. Although the women who replied were not a strictly random sample, their responses represent the views of a highly diverse population of women executives.

Six women, including the two coauthors, will lead you on a journey of exploration into the wonders of working around the world. Colorful stories from women who took up the challenge of working overseas will bring the international experience alive. Each story has its own lessons, and the experiences are particularly instructive when seen up close. As you get to know us, we hope you'll enjoy our stories and feel that you've learned from them – and maybe find that you have a few things in common with us.

We will share our secrets and strategies, such as how to use your feminine style to your advantage, how to be market-savvy and assignment-wise, and how to make a successful return. We want you to feel prepared to take off on your own international adventure, to leapfrog the competition, and to take heart through the inevitable challenges. There are a growing number of professional women with whom you can build bonds based on shared experiences. You will become part of an international network of like-minded "global girls" who have had their passports to success stamped time and time again. So, let's introduce you to some of these inspiring women:

- **Anna Catalano**, fluent in Mandarin, moved as a senior manager from Chicago to Beijing with a husband and two small children for two years while establishing Amoco's downstream office and exploring her Chinese roots. She later spent another five years abroad, this time in London as Group Vice President of Global Marketing for BP, and was recognized in *Fortune*'s 2001 "Most Powerful Women in International Business" before making the decision to walk away from it all in 2003 and spend time with her extended family in Texas. She now serves as an independent director on several public boards.

- **Diane Gulyas**, a chemical engineer with a passion for customers, had 10 years of experience when she went over two bosses' heads to request a position overseas in Geneva, Switzerland. She and her husband lived there for 2 ½ years and then transferred to Belgium, where she supervised a manufacturing plant for another year and a half before returning home to Wilmington, Delaware, to work directly with

DuPont's CEO. Recognized in *Fortune*'s 2006 "50 Most Powerful Women," she now manages an international staff of seventy-five hundred and a multibillion-dollar division of DuPont, one of the world's largest chemical companies.

- **Jacqualyn "Jackie" Fouse,** fluent in French, and with a good working knowledge of Spanish, German, and Italian, knew in her teenage years that she wanted to live and work internationally. Offered an opportunity to work for Alcon Laboratories in the headquarters of its parent company, Nestlé, in Vevey, Switzerland, she left Ft. Worth, Texas, as a solid middle manager in finance. For the next eight years, she worked for Nestlé and gained broad and significant business and financial experience until she was courted by Swissair Group's CEO to join as its Chief Financial Officer (CFO) and for one year helped manage the company through its bankruptcy. She returned home to Ft. Worth as senior vice president and CFO of Alcon Laboratories, a $5 billion division of Nestlé. She was awarded "Financial Executive of the Year" in 2005 by the Institute of Management Accountants and Robert Half International.

- **Patricia Kranz** studied Russian history and became proficient in the language before moving from Washington, D.C., to Moscow with no job but a strong gut feeling it was *the* place to be in the 1990s for a journalist. Her instincts proved correct, as she broke many stories, including eight cover stories about some of the most important events of the decade: the collapse of the Soviet Union and the building of post-Communist Russia. She spent a total of seven years in Russia and then, upon her return to New York, managed reporters in six European countries and then served as national news editor at *BusinessWeek*, before accepting her current role as deputy editor, Sunday Business Section, *New York Times*.

- **Perry Yeatman**, young, single, and a junior executive, left Baltimore, Maryland, for Singapore, where she began her expansive 10-year international career, moving up quickly in responsibility, title, and remuneration as she hopscotched from Singapore to Moscow and then to London. She parlayed her global contacts into a senior job with Unilever in Greenwich, Connecticut, where she worked for nearly four years. After a brief time-out to spend time with her new husband and daughter, she took a senior position at Kraft Foods, Inc., in Chicago. She now serves as senior vice president for international corporate affairs and global issues management. She is one of Kraft's top 50 executives and is responsible for corporate affairs in more than 100 countries. She is a published author.

- **Stacie Nevadomski Berdan**, who grew up traveling and wanted the added thrill of working in multiple cultures, moved from Burson-Marsteller's Washington, D.C., office to Hong Kong the day after her wedding. She spent three intense years in Asia at a critical juncture in her mid-level career and transitioned into a senior global position upon her return to Washington, D.C., jumping from vice president to global account managing director in just a few years. At the age of thirty-four, she was named a partner in WPP, Burson-Marsteller's parent company, and ranked in the top 1 percent of the largest marketing and communications conglomerate in the world. Searching for a more balanced life, she turned her substantial achievements in the fast-paced corporate world into a successful career as writer, speaker, and consultant. She is a mother of two and a published author of business literature.

These women have experience across industries. They have worked in a variety of countries in various roles for differing time periods, and they went abroad at different stages in their personal lives. Their combined experience should encourage you. Their successes should instill you with a "can-do" attitude to start preparing for your own adventure. Come along with us as we retrace their footsteps so that you, too, can reap the personal and professional rewards that come from working internationally.

Making It Real

In my three years in Asia, I grew both professionally and personally. From getting used to being the only woman in a room full of Japanese men to managing the cultural divide between myself and my team of twenty-five Hong Kong Chinese to managing multiple currencies, cultures, and business protocols – sometimes in a single day – I faced challenges I had never faced before. But not only did I manage them, I also excelled in these situations –

13

admittedly surprising both myself and the management team back home. It wasn't just the big things that mattered. There can be as much a sense of triumph from just arriving on time for a meeting when you don't know Korean and the taxi driver speaks no English as from landing that big contract. After all, if you can't get to the meeting, you can't land the contract. My business savvy, management skills, and stature within the company increased quickly, as did my title and salary.

— **Stacie, coauthor and consultant**

I cannot think of any other single experience that has contributed more to both my professional and my personal development than living overseas.

— **Jackie, Alcon**

I witnessed two of the most dramatic moments in history in Russia, and I will never forget them. Career-wise, I made great strides by writing story after story about Russia's struggles to create a market economy.

— **Patricia, *New York Times***

Having international experience as a woman allows you to be measured in a different way: you are competing on a much more level playing field.

— **Anna, former BP Executive**

As a senior leader and member of the executive management team at DuPont who spent twenty-five years moving up the ranks, I have one strong piece of advice for women here and in business in general: Go overseas. It will make a huge, positive difference in your career. Do it after you've been in the business for 5 to 10 years, so that you can reap the benefits and rewards for a longer time throughout your career, as well as avoid some of the complexities that usually come later in life, such as marriage, children, and aging parents.

— **Diane, DuPont**

The Twenty-First-Century Global Marketplace

These women have witnessed first-hand the transformations shaping business today. More and more companies want to succeed in the increasingly global marketplace, if not to become global leaders. Companies that once gave lip service to "being close to customers worldwide" are now gearing up to make that commitment real, while companies that have always had extensive international operations are expanding them. They are searching the world for the best resources at the best prices and selling to consumers around the globe. Knowledge and understanding of foreign cultures, regulations, economies, consumer preferences, and work habits are now critical to corporate survival.

The nature and pace of competition are also changing. Businesses are competing at every level— sourcing, manufacturing, distribution, marketing, sales, and customer service – in various markets. As the global business environment becomes more competitive, companies recognize that they can best compete if they have a diverse leadership team with a rich mix of skills, perspectives, and experiences. This opportunity is important because it can help overcome the hurdles business women still face today.

The Reality of Women in Business Today

Obstacles remain in the way of women's progress. Let's take the United States as an example. Although the number of women in managerial and administrative positions has increased steadily since 1946 (from 5 percent to 38 percent), the percentage of the whole has remained constant (U.S. Department of Labor statistics). Women in middle management positions seem to be stuck there, not making it to the top nearly as often as their male counter-parts. And despite what you hear, the pay gap still exists: women earn about 75 cents to every dollar a man makes.

This discrepancy is even more remarkable in light of the fact that the number of women earning MBAs has doubled in the past twenty years and just recently surpassed men (U.S. Department of Education statistics). In the past, women's limited participation in management was commonly attributed to their failure to pursue advanced degrees – or, it was argued, to their earning degrees in the liberal arts, not business. Well, that's certainly not true now, but it wasn't true then either: in most industries, mid-level managers did not have MBAs but rather rose from the shop floor or from junior-level positions. Historically, women have not been brought along this promotional chain at the same rate.

However, thanks to the courageous women who have been pushing

15

for gender equality in business over the past 30 years, women have made significant strides – many of them quite recently. In fact, two-thirds of the 12 women currently heading Fortune 500 companies have achieved that seat of power since 2001. Although the number of women in senior leadership positions still pales in comparison – 488 men lead the rest of the Fortune 500 – a new day *is* dawning.

The dawn of this new day highlights the working mothers, professional women who have children and remain in the workforce. Going overseas can be especially potent and powerful as these women navigate the maze of "balance" and "having it all" and settle on what works best for them personally and professionally. Going overseas opens doors and provides options. Many times, women with children choose to exit the career highway, allowing their careers to take a back seat to childrearing. Being a new globetrotter actually helps in this respect, whether you choose to take time off, go part-time, or even go international.

First, leaving work or scaling back becomes much easier if you've achieved higher pay and faster promotions because of your time overseas. By compressing more career growth into the years before you have kids, you have many more options and thus direct benefits after they are born. **Second**, international credentials make it more likely that you can make a financial go of a part-time career during peak "mommy" years. Faster salary increases and promotions make it easier to save more money while you are overseas, banking for the future. **Third**, if you choose to go abroad with children, you can often afford better childcare and domestic help than at home. And, of course, there is always the argument that taking your kids with you is the best thing you can do for them, depending on the stage in their development when it happens.

Making It Real

For a woman, international work experience gives us a demonstrated record of flexibility and versatility that helps overcome the generalizations of how women work and what we want and/or don't want. It gives us the chance to show that we can work in different, difficult, and often dangerous environments that often earns us a second look when they're evaluating candidates for new jobs or promotions or high-profile assignments. It adds the "how'd she do that?" element to our resumes.

– Donna, former U.S. Ambassador to Brazil, Venezuela, Bolivia, and the Dominican Republic

---

A Few Words About Gender Stereotyping...

Gender stereotyping is defined as a shared set of beliefs about purported qualities of females and males in a particular group. A great deal of research in the United States over the past 10 years indicates that gender stereotyping within the corporate environment continues to be one of several contributing factors limiting the advancement of women. The goal of this book is to offer advice to women on how to overcome some of these obstacles with a practical, relevant approach. The majority of women we interviewed a) believe that women and men are treated differently in the workplace, b) are fully aware that most research studies comparing the *competencies* of male and female managers have found the differences negligible, and c) have chosen to leverage their femaleness into a competitive advantage. For example, over the years women have been told they are "too soft" for leadership positions and need an iron fist or a "command-and-control" style with which to rule. However, in cross-cultural situations, emotional intelligence, team building, and collaboration are critical to success – much more often than an iron fist. Women are using differences such as these to develop their own winning leadership style. Gender stereotyping exists in all aspects of our society, so we shouldn't be surprised to find it present in the business environment. Whether it is left over from the "bad old days" or has some basis in childrearing decisions, we find that globetrotting helps no matter what.

The Advantages of Being a Woman Overseas

In researching this book, we uncovered some interesting trends. It seems that many of the traits now deemed critical to business success in the international marketplace are also emerging as the critical ones for tomorrow's great leaders: adaptability, team building, and inclusiveness. In addition, good communication and listening skills, cross-cultural competence, and the ability to influence, inspire, and motivate despite conflict and stress serve business leaders well.

Making It Real

In some cultures, men are uneasy with a senior woman. I always look for ways to put those people at ease. There is a "powership" struggle between men and women at times, and I try my best not to be intimidating or threatening so that we can all work together. I over-communicate why we need to work together, and most of the time it works. A woman's natural style gives us the advantage to be aware of and adapt to other people's positions and perspectives.

– Jackie, Alcon

In the U.S., women traditionally tried to be "just like men" in the workplace, with mixed degrees of success and often a fair amount of internal emotional turmoil. But in the vast majority of overseas markets, being a woman can work in your favor. So don't deny your instincts and socialization – use them!

– Perry, coauthor and Kraft Foods, Inc.

As a journalist sometimes it was useful that the Russians never considered women to have powerful jobs – you could blend into the scenery more and hear things maybe they didn't want you to hear or see things they didn't want you to see.

– Patricia, *New York Times*

According to research on gender differences and management style, this "new" type of leadership is not actually new at all. In fact, many professional women – as well as a host of academics – argue that this style is the way women have been leading and managing for years. The news from our survey is that in most markets around the world, leadership styles traditionally considered feminine in the U.S. can be far more effective than those considered to be masculine.

The New Globetrotters Survey:
Women and the International Experience

The vast majority of women who took our global online survey agreed that there are common traits considered most critical for success in working internationally. The majority chose the following five, listed here in no particular order:

- Adaptability and flexibility
- Ability to listen and communicate well
- Skill at building teams and relationships
- Patience and persistence (a complementary twosome)
- Curiosity and open-mindedness

Additional traits that gave a strong showing included the ability to inspire and motivate, take risks, make decisions, and exhibit emotional intelligence. It is important to note that these traits are all more classically "female" than "male." Let us briefly expand on the five, based on our survey results.

Adaptability and flexibility: A fluid, non-rigid style that appreciates cultural differences and local knowledge and understands that there may be more than one way to get things done. An ability to tolerate high degrees of ambiguity and work well under pressure is critical because of the surprises and difficult circumstances that regularly occur in unfamiliar environments.

Making It Real

Style flexing is an important trait for people who work overseas. It goes beyond the ability to adapt to a new environment; it enables you to instinctively connect with people of all cultures. Whether counseling the USAID Administrator on media strategies in Islamabad, explaining U.S. brand standards to 500 NGO workers in Nairobi, or delivering textbooks to schoolgirls in Baghdad, I always assess the audience first, determine their level of interest and understanding, and then adapt not only my message but my delivery – volume, tone, and gestures. Finding the right mix is key to making an instant connection.

– Joanne, USAID

Ability to listen and communicate well: This skill also entails reading between the lines, intuiting nonverbal clues, and interpreting the environment. Empathy and the ability to understand others' perspectives play a critical role in establishing trust, understanding, and mutual respect. Differences in language, culture, politics, and religion – to name just a few –

increase the likelihood of miscommunication between global citizens and local teams. An established and accepted good communication style builds a bank of goodwill to apply against future mishaps. Expatriates often need local knowledge and know-how much more than they think. If your style is to lead by command and control, you may never learn what you need to know because your local staff, clients, and colleagues may never tell you. If you lead with an interactive and inclusive approach – which, by the way, does not mean being weak or indecisive – you will be more likely to encourage local employees, clients, and colleagues to speak up and help you make the best decisions. Both styles are decisive and strong, but their effects on teams, and therefore the business results, are different.

Making It Real

I've seen so many expats (mostly male) crash and burn in China because they were flying blind without local team knowledge, mainly because they appeared to the team to be too arrogant to want their insights.

– Rebecca, consultant

Working abroad requires a higher level of listening skills than you may have ever thought you needed. You must not only listen with your ears and hear what is being said, but you must also pay attention equally to what is **not** being said – the body language, gestures, and overall impression you are giving and receiving.

– Stacie, coauthor and consultant

Skill at building teams and relationships: Understanding that getting to know people as individuals – appreciating who they are in order to work effectively with them – enhances your ability to succeed manifold. Building teams and creating an atmosphere of esprit de corps will have a great impact. Knowing when and where to take charge, as well as how to share power, information, and decision making, makes a difference.

Making It Real

Despite the difference in cultures and customs, people are a lot more alike than we think. Great leaders' skills transcend culture.

– Anna, former BP executive

Patience and persistence: Understand that things take time and operate on "local" time, whatever that may mean in the various markets. Don't rush things or demand immediate answers, respect, or change. More like the heat of the sun than the force of the wind, international leaders focus on long-term success, as opposed to the gratification of instant results, being rewarded with more balance and less frustration. Local teams admire and respect leaders who take the time to get to know them, their culture, and their local market.

Making It Real

I was the first female plant supervisor in Europe. It was daunting to be leading an all-male factory, especially since I was replacing a local who was retiring. I didn't speak the language and hadn't lived in Belgium before. My company took a risk in sending me, and I took a crazy risk in going. But I was patient with myself and my team, soaking up their knowledge and figuring out, with their help, how best to share mine. It paid off. Together, we improved operations manifold, and we won awards for our outstanding work in just 18 months.

– Diane, DuPont

After enduring so much work in the UK, I've learned to be patient and stay the course. It now takes a lot to rattle my cage.

– Lisa, VogtGoldstein

Curiosity and open-mindedness: Open-minded people enjoy the overseas experience for its breadth of newness and for the sheer joy of operating in an environment outside their comfort zone. The ability to deal with differences in culture as well as infrastructure – be it the workings of the financial industry or local public transportation – while doing the job at hand requires the ability to enjoy risk and the spirit of adventure. Being open in dealing with whatever comes your way builds strong teams, teaches employees by example, and helps you learn the relevant ropes faster. Leaders learn more abroad if they are willing to let go of the status quo and fully experience being overseas.

Making It Real

Working abroad allows you to see both the best and the worst in

21

a country, a culture, or an individual. Try not to get too frustrated with it because every coin has two sides.

– **Jackie, Alcon**

So, how do you use these traits to your advantage, especially while working abroad? Read on, for in Chapters 5 through 8, we illustrate how numerous women have turned their feminine traits into a competitive advantage while working overseas.

Comments from Women on the Front Line

Our global, online survey respondents represented all regions: approximately 66 % from North America, 19 % from Europe, 13 % from Asia-Pacific, and 2 % from Latin America. The respondents' ages ranged from twenty-five to sixty-five.

The majority of women surveyed loved the challenge, the adventure, and the professional and personal growth inherent in international work. To be sure, going global presented some significant challenges. But the rewards were even greater: mastering new skills, solving problems they would not have encountered back home, and boosting their self-confidence several notches. Succeeding overseas added other dimensions to their character and opened both professional and personal doors that they probably would never have encountered otherwise. As part of the survey, women were asked to provide comments (all anonymously). Here's one that sums up what many had to say.

> There is no doubt that having responsibility across multiple countries has made a significant impact on my ability to secure great roles and progress at a much faster rate. There is a general perception that if you have worked (or lived or traveled) overseas, then your outlook on life and the way you perceive things around you and your acceptance of differences in people is going to be greater than those who have only operated within one market.

The vast majority of the women surveyed (83 percent) cited their experience working and living internationally as a key reason for their rapid advancement. Contrary to assumptions in many companies that women will not do well overseas, our survey indicates that women usually excel.

Most survey participants stated that being female gave them an advantage in many countries, specifically because there were no "rules" to follow. Traditional male roles simply didn't apply as new ground was being broken. Read on for more insight from our survey respondents as they completed the following open-ended statement, "Succeeding in international business is different for women because...."

> In many countries, women are treated differently than men. You have to understand the differences and figure out how to use them to your advantage.

> When a competent professional American female goes abroad, her local colleagues notice that she is female, but in most cases, do not mentally classify her with their local female co-workers. They either classify her strictly as a high-status professional (deserving respect), or they are unsure how to classify her because she is outside their range of experience.

> I was more easily accepted as a woman in business in Russia, the UK, Kazakhstan, and Serbia than in the U.S.A.

> Women in general, regardless of geographical location, need to utilize a different set of skills than men in order to create a successful position within an internationally oriented organization.

> Women must deal with two types of stereotypes: one [regarding] nationality and the other [related to] being a woman. Moreover, women are better equipped to deal with the cultural differences due to the inherent strengths of [their] feminine characteristics.

> Men often overestimate their capabilities, and this leads to hubris and failure, while women [tend to] underestimate their[s]. [T]his means they are less likely to even try, but when they do, they are more likely to succeed.

Many of our respondents were among the "firsts" in their organizations to go abroad, e.g., the first woman sent overseas, the first to the region, the first to the country, the first as an office or plant manager, or the first married woman with children. As such they didn't have the luxury of role models. In an article in *The Wall Street Journal* (July 24, 2006) Archer Daniels Midland (ADM) CEO Patricia Woertz, who took on her first big operations job for Chevron, Canada, moving to Vancouver from California in a matter of days, noted something about her climb: she never held a job that had previously been held by a woman. Pioneers must want to be groundbreakers and must have a sense of adventure. Great rewards usually demand high risk.

Global Track as Fast Track

Despite the risky, wild rides that many women had during their postings abroad, almost all agreed that the experience accelerated their careers. They cited benefits such as enhanced professional growth, the establishment of high-level business contacts, and the ability to take on general and line management jobs earlier in their careers. For most, advancement came rapidly.

Most women reported numerous professional advantages to being female. For example, they described themselves as being highly visible – because they were women and foreign – and they leveraged it to the best of their ability. People were curious to meet them and granted them instant credibility – assuming they were the best in their field because they were women sent by successful multinational companies. Why would such international organizations send anyone but the best overseas?

Making It Real

Moving and working overseas greatly enhanced my earning power. It also vaulted me into more senior positions with higher profiles than if I had stayed in Canada or the United States. Who wouldn't go overseas?!

– Penny, ABN AMRO

My years of working abroad catapulted my career. Succeeding in situations that were difficult, renewing my confidence, and leading to recognition by leadership directly affected my consideration for advancement and management positions. I differentiated myself considerably from my peers with whom I'd be competing in the years to come. I moved up quickly – being promoted essentially every eighteen to twenty-four months as opposed to the standard three to five years.

– Diane, DuPont

I was promoted literally overnight from a Grade 20 to a Grade 25 position, a jump so large it required permission from my company's global board of directors. Permission was granted, and I made a huge leap – essentially doubling my salary – all because the company's China president lobbied so hard for it. It would never have happened in the States. I was in the right place – overseas – at the right time.

– Rebecca, consultant

In this day and age, going overseas is not just an option – it's a necessity.

– Sheila, Barclays Bank

If you love a challenge and if you thrive on beating the odds and delivering the goods on budget and ahead of schedule, and then relish the opportunity for another challenge, even tougher than the one before, going overseas may be for you. So pack your bags and join us on our journey illustrating how you, too, can fast-track your career by going global.

D.

Chapter 2

Is Going Global Right for You?

I went to Hong Kong as a newly married mid-manager. It was a risky proposition to leave the comforts of my established position in Washington, D.C., but I wanted to be more than just a D.C. insider. That risk was compounded by the fact that I would begin married life in an Asian city, even though at the time it was still a British colony. Some days were extremely difficult, but I stuck to it. I grew to love Hong Kong and understand and admire my local team. I will always appreciate my husband for agreeing to participate in what proved to be a fulfilling and fun three years.

— Stacie, coauthor and consultant

No matter what the research and women themselves say, only you can decide whether a global assignment is right for you. It can be the best thing for your career, or the worst thing for your personal life – or both, or neither! It all depends on your circumstances and how you approach the decision-making process. Whether you decide to move abroad or pursue an international career operating from home base, the rewards can be great – different, but great either way.

Do You Have the Right Stuff?

Before you read the list below, think about a time in your personal or professional life when you felt stretched and challenged. Ask yourself the following ten questions:

* Do you have a real sense of adventure? Do you enjoy the unknown, the different, and the unexpected?

27

- Do you operate well outside your comfort zone, even if you are feeling alone and isolated from all things normal for you?

- Do you thrive on diversity – language, ethnicity, religion, currency, culture, social norms, foods, politics – lots of it and all at the same time?

- Do you like being in charge, even in constantly changing tides? Can you survive – even lead – among chaos and confusion?

- Are you curious – deep-down *interested* – in what makes the world go round?

- Would you consider yourself extremely flexible?

- Can you build relationships, even if you have to communicate in your or someone else's second language?

- Are you willing to go the extra mile and follow through by using the right mix of diplomacy and persistence?

- Do you know how to really listen? Can you read between the lines and understand what is being said even if the faces you're reading look like blank pages – and vice versa, i.e., when the facial expressions are clear but the words are confusing?

- Can you handle failure and learn from it? Can you keep it in perspective? Do you have a sense of humor about it?

If you answered "yes" or even "somewhat" to the majority of these questions, working internationally could be a viable option for you.

Making It Real

For me, the wanderlust set in early. When I was a child, I read books about people and places all over the world, and I could picture myself doing wonderful things in these faraway lands.

– Penny, ABN AMRO

I first decided I wanted to live overseas at 13 years of age. It was during a class trip to Europe. I had never been abroad before but loved it: the architecture, the museums, the food, the people, and, yes, I admit I loved the royalty, the pageantry, and the grandeur of it. London especially captured my heart. It was more than just the hope of one day being "Princess Perry" – though being a senior executive in a Fortune 50 company was probably further from my mind than acquiring a royal title at that point in my life.

– Perry, coauthor and Kraft Foods, Inc.

If you don't like to fly; if moving away from friends and family frightens you; if you are afraid of failure; if you think "different" is synonymous with "bad;" if you prefer things to be black and white, not gray; if finding a new hairdresser, new doctor, or new favorite shoe store concerns you, living abroad is probably not for you. But if you are willing to deal with the sacrifices, they will turn out to be a small price to pay for the greater return in personal and professional growth. Let's take a look at a few of the little things some women missed while on their international tour of duty: "I missed…

…Mom's homemade chocolate chip cookies."

…Saturday night movies with the girls back home."

…driving my own car."

…favorite family recipes calling for unique American ingredients like Velveeta."

…being able to buy clothes off the rack because I was not the standard size."

If you are willing to give up some personal pleasures and creature comforts for a few years, a world of excitement awaits. The vast majority of women who have lived and worked overseas are glad they did.

If you are thinking, "I could never move because of this or that personal circumstance," keep those thoughts at bay for now. Do yourself a big favor and do **not** assume that you cannot move for personal reasons alone. With the right planning, knowledge, and a leap of faith, it could be one of the wisest moves you ever made.

Thinking Globally

The next step in determining if going global is right for you involves beginning to think internationally. Doing so is critical to determining whether you would enjoy being surrounded by things foreign for several years.

- **Watch the BBC** instead of CNN or your local nightly news – or better yet, watch them both and compare the different perspectives and priorities.

- **Read international newspapers and magazines,** such as The *Economist* and The *International Herald Tribune* for Americans; The *New York Times* if you live outside the United States – or even if you live outside New York City.

- **Read foreign newspapers and periodicals** from the regions and countries that interest you most; there is usually an English-language version that you can access online. Subscribe to a daily newspaper in a language you can read.

- **Practice your foreign language,** especially for business conversation.

- **Practice your English** if it is your second language; it remains the language of international business.

- **Travel abroad** on a personal vacation.

- **Identify international groups or organizations** in your area and explore how you might get involved – or at least participate enough to expose yourself to other cultures.

Making It Real

In addition to experiencing, learning about, and adapting to another culture, you also see your home country from a different perspective. This new perspective can be quite enlightening, and it's something you retain even after you move back. I think it makes you a more discerning individual.

– Jackie, Alcon

After working six months with little or no sleep on a grueling assignment for a client, I decided to take an extended vacation – in Hong Kong. I had done a semester abroad in London and had traveled much of Europe, but had never been to Asia. I stayed with an American friend working on the new Hong Kong International Airport. We traveled to Guilin, China; sailed down the Yangshuo River; and even survived a class 8 typhoon in Macau. What impressed me most, however, was the lifestyle of the young expats I met; everybody had a fascinating job and a fantastic flat. I was working twelve to fourteen hours a day in Manhattan and paying $1300/month to live in four hundred square feet. In the game of life, the overseas professionals seemed to be winning. I wanted to live the life of an expat: work hard, play hard,

and have the company pay my rent! Five months after that vacation, I was living and working in Asia.

– **Joanne, USAID**

To all women considering taking an international position and
moving abroad, I say, "Do it!" Working and living abroad provides a level of experience that 99 percent of your peers will never achieve. It gives you a boost, an added dimension to your skill
set, because you will have a "world-view" or approach to solving
problems. Most organizations find this skill rare – and priceless.

– **Pamela, Westinghouse**

Living Abroad vs. the Constant Traveler

To live the life of an expatriate or that of the road warrior – that is the
question. Naturally, there are pros and cons to both. Traveling a great deal
takes its toll on your body and your family (if applicable) but doesn't involve the upheaval of a physical move. You won't have to worry about
selling, buying, or renting a house or apartment. You won't have to go
through the angst of what to pack, what to store – and, yes, what to throw
out. You won't have to worry about whether your household goods will
arrive at their destination, or about setting up house in a foreign land that
doesn't have your accustomed appliances or groceries. You won't have to
miss your friends, and if you can macromanage your international travel
schedule, you probably won't have to miss weddings, funerals, and other
big events. However, you also won't experience as revolutionary a change.
As a professional you will likely be judged as ethnocentric whether or not
you are. If you have a "global role," you will not be expected to understand too much of what is going on in any particular country, as you are
expected to bring big-picture solutions, not market-specific plans that
solve local problems. You will be perceived as an expert from HQ, someone to be respected and listened to, though perhaps not always welcomed
or trusted because "you don't live here and you don't get it."

For many professionals, having an international career while working
at home base is the optimal choice. For some, their careers simply took
off this way and although they may have been afforded the opportunity to
move overseas, they declined for personal reasons. Some did not want to
give up a seat so close to decision-making power, viewing their proximity

as a better position for their advancement. This can certainly be true. Many times, however, the only way a new manager can acquire international skills is to take the risk and move abroad.

Following is a snapshot of the major differences between the two. You decide what's best for you.

Living Abroad PROS:	Living Abroad CONS:
Greater career-related rewards and recognition, through financial gains or higher positions	Danger of being "out-of-sight, out-of-mind" with respect to HQ
Exponential personal and professional growth	Initial culture shock and adaptation for self (and family members)
Differentiation within current and future organizations Intense, confidence-building environment	Long hours and stress related to working multiple time zones: yours and HQ's
Fun, adventure-filled and mind-expanding travel opportunities	Different and inconsistent healthcare, foreign school systems, and potential pollution concerns
New friends for life and special shared experiences	Missing friends, family, and many big life events
Enhanced communication and problem-solving skills	Feeling isolated and alone
Global Travel PROS:	**Global Travel CONS:**
Global perspective for your organization	Lack of immersion and depth in the country and culture
Usually a position at seat of power and where decision making takes place	Danger of addressing the problems topically without truly understanding local situation
Respected as an expert from HQ in local markets – but at a distance	Relationships take much longer to build and maintain
Less personal upheaval	Lots of jet lag and travel-related stress, including long stretches of time away from family and friends

Making It Real

If you are perceived as just "parachuting" in from time to time, you will miss building the necessary bridges and contacts with the local staff. Moreover, you will not experience the full richness of living in a different culture. Understanding local customs will enhance your effectiveness in your job, and the only true way to do that is to live abroad. And you know, the view from the center is never quite the same as it is from the outside.

– Penny, ABN AMRO

Overall, the vast majority of women and human resource executives we interviewed agree that although you can usually do your job effectively while traveling in and out of countries, you miss the deep dive if you don't go overseas – at least for a portion of your career. The new globetrotters tend to work and live abroad for at least three years and, if possible, return to an international or global position as their next move. Here's what some of our surveyed women have to say about going global.

Women Who Know Say...

- 85% agree that their international experience accelerated their careers
- 78% agree that it had a significant, positive impact on compensation
- 71% agree they were given greater responsibility earlier in their career because of their international assignments
- 49% first went abroad to work in the beginning of their career, 31% as middle managers, 15% as senior executives, 5% as executive management
- 73% lived abroad for more than four years
- 53% lived in more than three countries

Source: The New Globetrotters Survey 2006

Be Prepared – We're Women!

Once you've determined the kind of international experience you'd like to have, you should begin preparing yourself for the resistance you will probably encounter when you begin to express your desire to go overseas. Women remain a distinct minority in the international business arena. You may be surprised by the seemingly ridiculous questions being asked of you – questions that have nothing to do with your skills or capabilities but everything to do with the fact that you are a woman. **Whether we like it or not, business is still dominated by men**. Both in the steps leading up to and your acceptance of an international assignment, you will probably not be treated the same as your male colleagues, even if you both go through the "same" process. Here are some of the comments we've heard from women about others' initial reactions to their international posting.

"Does your husband know that you are considering moving?"

"You're the only woman here. What do we do with you?"

"Are you having marital problems?"

"I think your husband should be here while we discuss the financials."

"No, really, which company transferred your husband?" (pause) "You're not married?"

Take heart! Know that many women have gone before you blazing trails, changing the way women are perceived around the world in business, and proving the gender skeptics wrong. Most women state that they were able to use their feminine skills and competencies toward greater rewards and results.

Timing Is Everything: Your Professional Status

Only you can determine the best time. The majority of the women who took our survey moved in the beginning of their careers, and it seems to have worked out successfully for them. We believe that any age or level works and that it all depends on your personal preference and situation. Here's a snapshot of what it might be like for you, according to your professional level.

For the Recent Graduate

While you're still **in college**, study abroad for at least one semester. Although studying outside your home country is different from working, it will help you find out if you actually like living abroad. You will learn how to buy food, use public transportation, set up personal systems such as phone and computer connections, and deal with local bureaucracies.

Many people get hooked on working internationally after studying abroad.

Once you have your degree, you'll also have your ambitions, and most likely a foreign language or two to your credit. Unless you have a specialist degree, prior overseas experience, or high-demand language skills, such as Arabic or Mandarin, you will probably find it quite competitive to be hired for an overseas post right out of school. International relocations are expensive, and therefore, the company wants a particular level of value for its investment. According to a recent *Fortune* article, 42 percent of the top thirty business schools in the United States reported an increased number of recruiters targeting students for overseas jobs (April 18, 2006). However, sometimes these recruiters are looking to hire the 30 percent of international students on campus for jobs back home. In any event, it's not impossible to land an international job right out of school, so go ahead and give it a try.

The other way to pursue an international career is to move yourself. Many "global souls" we know finished school, worked a little, and then took off to see the world with the intention of getting the "travel bug" out of their system before returning to a corporate career. Some did just that, but others settled in one place, established themselves, and were taken in by multinationals as local hires. Most of the time, companies will help you get the necessary paperwork to work for them, especially since you will be a less-expensive "local hire." This can be a great way to complement your academic work with real on-the-ground experience in a foreign country.

Since you will not have had any formal business training, you will be shaped and molded primarily by the international experience. As a result, you will soak up a different array of skills – particularly those that are needed in your new country, culture, and industry. While you may not acquire cutting-edge professional skills if you are in a developing market or one that is not considered a leader in your field, the amount you learn will move you well ahead of your peers back home. It will be necessary, however, for you to find a mentor who has international experience, whether male or female. He or she can assist you in understanding exactly what types of professional skills are necessary in your field – that you may not be learning – to compete with your peers. While your atypical experiences will be an asset, you can't be so different that leaders can't place you in an organization, especially if you want to continue to advance.

Making It Real

Right out of school, I worked in Africa for almost five years, gaining a lot of experience and building up my self-confidence. When I returned to the U.S. and began my job hunt, I found that people did not know how to react to a confident 27-year-old with extensive international work experience. Some assumed I had exaggerated my role. A few stared at me in disbelief, while others disregarded the work I had done in Africa as trivial since it was not done "here." I learned very quickly that most people did not have a frame of reference for my global advanced experience and could not appreciate my skill set. I revised my job search and landed a great position with an international company that understood the value I brought to the table.

– Jeanne, human resource training consultant

I moved to Russia right out of college. I had studied Russian and was religious about learning the language, taking index cards with me to practice everywhere I went. I even sat in front of the TV and mimicked what was being said, even if I didn't understand it! It was a great way to pick up the accent and proper pronunciation.

– Nancy, Handelsbank

For the Junior Executive

As a junior executive you have a few years of experience. That will have tempered your hubris enough to recognize that you don't have all the answers, but you will still be cocky enough to think you can find them. You probably aren't very expensive (i.e., your salary is low), as you aren't yet very high up on the organizational ladder, but you've been targeted as a "rising star" or one to watch and have undergone some professional development training or other career-enhancing investments by the company. You have enough depth that HR is actively tracking your career and monitoring your progress, and there could be real commitment on both your sides to make an international assignment a possibility.

Once abroad, you will have an opportunity to make an impact. You will have enough skills to make a difference, yet not enough experience to impede your ability to be flexible and learn how to do things with a twist: in other words, a solid skill set combined with an ability to see new oppor-

36

tunities and ways of doing things more effectively or efficiently. You will have the distinct advantage of having local market peers looking to you to exchange knowledge.

Making It Real

I studied Chinese language and history at Yale, which requires a senior thesis. For that, I spent four months in Taiwan conducting research between my junior and senior years and was hooked on the complexities of Chinese politics. After graduating, I started freelancing for the [U.S.] State Department's International Visitors Program, honing my language skills and then working for them as a Chinese interpreter. Two years later, I took a job in Qingdao teaching English for a year, then spent another year traveling and updating a popular China travel guide. I was in Guangzhou on June 4, 1989, when the tanks rolled in Beijing. Watching that sad and complex piece of history unfold around me was a life-changing experience, though after a lot of soul-searching, it only deepened my commitment to playing my part in China's transformation. I've been able to do just that working for two multinationals in the PRC for a combined six years and now as a U.S.-based consultant helping companies learn how to determine their most successful China strategy.

– Rebecca, consultant

My first international assignment was in Jakarta, Indonesia. I was twenty-six years old. I had previously proven myself on a few difficult client assignments, and PWC and I both agreed that a one-to-two month stint would be a great next project for me. I thought it would be a great way to test the international waters. Well, the project ran over and evolved into an eleven-month assignment that was deemed so successful that I was asked to take on another assignment right after it in the Philippines, "since I was in the region." As a result, my international career was off and running long before I would have expected.

– Laura, IBM Consulting

For Those in Middle Management

As a professional in middle management, you probably have between eight and fifteen years of experience depending on your industry, your academic background, and your on-the-job training. More likely than not, you have achieved a certain degree of status or standing within your company and are looking for a way to distinguish yourself from your peers as the upstream channel grows increasingly narrow. You view an overseas assignment as an opportunity to do just that. Although it may be a bit worrisome being away from home base and the decision makers there, you will be taking on new and challenging projects almost every day, learning things your peers won't have the chance to learn back home.

As a middle manager abroad, you will most likely be a big fish in a small to medium-sized pond. You may have line management responsibility and a profit-and-loss (P&L) role. Unless you are moving to an overseas HQ, you will probably be one of the most senior managers in the office and will be expected to perform the duties that a senior manager does: lead, manage, serve as the public face of the company, solve problems, and have most – if not all – the answers. Your professional advancement can really take off at this point as you deliver results while learning how to do business as a global leader outside your home base.

Making It Real

I went overseas mid-career, which I recommend. My combination of significant experience to date, in-depth knowledge of my company, and a level of sophistication that only comes with age all made it much easier for me to figure things out. Whether I was trying to determine how to negotiate the best deal for my company, how to evade the numerous shots of vodka at regular banquets I attended, how to buy anything in the Russian version of a grocery store, or navigate the Moscow subway system, I felt much better prepared.

– **Pamela, Westinghouse**

I left Stockholm for Chicago mid-career, and I think it's a very good time to go. Professionally, I was senior enough to significantly contribute with my experience, background and thinking, but I didn't have to take on complete responsibility for a department and budget. Therefore I had room to grow. Personally, it was perfect timing for my family as my children were young (4 ½ and 2 when the adventure began), so they quickly adapted to their new environment.

– **Annica, Kraft Foods, Inc.**

I had never seriously considered moving overseas when I was tapped by top management at ExxonMobil as someone who should go on international tour of duty to gain broader experience. I was a senior manager in my late thirtiess, and I moved to Belgium with my new husband; we'd been married about a month. He was supportive, and I was happy to take on new challenges. Well, I got them! I worked out of our European HQ, was assigned to financial reporting and then customer service – two functions for which I had no experience – and during my customer service role had five hundred people working for me, with representation in almost every European country. Talk about sweaty palms! I learned so much about managing diverse working styles and cultures that I now am a much broader thinker and better manager for the experience.

– **Rebecca, ExxonMobil**

For the Senior Executive

As a senior executive, you are probably considering moving overseas for one of two reasons. The first is that your company now requires international experience in order for you to move up to executive management. The second is that you've always wanted to go overseas but could never manage the personal aspects of moving your life and family abroad. Perhaps now the kids have moved out or are in college. High-performing senior executives with excellent track records will go overseas under certain conditions – most times if they are their own boss.

As a senior executive, you will have a different type of adjustment ahead of you. First of all, you are most likely older and wiser and possibly more set in your ways. You'll want to make sure you can adjust by taking an extended site visit to the location you are considering. Moving abroad takes a great deal of energy and commitment. Make sure you have both. In addition, more will be expected of you, as you will be a senior representative from HQ, and you will most likely have a high-profile position with large internal and external responsibilities. You will have more flexibility, more decision-making authority, significant credibility to enable you to go out on a limb, and, most likely, an expat package that will ensure your personal comfort. You will be expected to hit the ground running fast. As a senior executive, the two most important things you can do are these: 1) do not assume you know everything because of your experience and 2) put your whole heart and soul into it right from the start so your local staff doesn't think you're there on early retirement – or worse on a golden parachute to get you out of HQ.

Making It Real

Although I had traveled and worked extensively overseas, I had never lived outside the U.S. I wanted to be part of this emerging global world for both professional and personal reasons. While I knew it would improve my capabilities as a consultant, I was honestly more drawn by a desire to expand my horizons and experience new things. At the time I moved to Paris, I was a member of the executive management team of Burson-Marsteller (the first woman on the company's worldwide management board), and many of my colleagues were surprised that I wanted to leave the U.S. You know, there are several paths you can take to expand your horizons: you can reinvent yourself and change your career totally … or you can trade one employer for another in the same industry in search of new opportunities … or you may find new opportunities within the same company. I did the latter and was extremely fortunate to be able to broaden my experiences and expand my universe.

– Barbara, strategy and innovation consultant

Timing Is Everything: Your Personal Status

Just as there are pros and cons to going overseas at various professional levels, the same holds true for personal status. Whether you're single, married, with kids, or not, women have done it before and have lessons to share with you. Here's a snapshot of what it might be like at the various stages of your personal life.

If You're Single

Women have told us that, "Being single in a foreign land can be wonderful and awful at the same time." It can be exhilarating and thrilling. It can be lonely. You can focus on your job and fine-tune your skills. You can work too much. It can be difficult to meet people, make friends, and date. But the friends you do make will probably be your lifelong best friends. If you do not deal well with loneliness or if you have suffered homesickness in your life (camp, college, or even moving out of your parents' house), moving to a foreign place may be overwhelming.

One of the benefits of being single is the speed at which you integrate. Out of necessity, most singles develop a group of friends that serves the function of a supportive, caring family. Most get out there and become involved in activities right away. Most single women who have lived abroad have the same comment about their life abroad: "I made the best friends of my life."

Making It Real

Before I moved to Singapore, I'd never even been to a movie alone – let alone ever felt lonely. In New York I lived with my college boyfriend and had a large group of friends. But I moved to Singapore not knowing a soul. Socially, the first few weeks were hard: no one to shop with on weekends or to grab a drink with after work. But soon I realized it's much easier to make new friends living overseas than it is back home; each single woman must replace her core group of gal pals, so there's a lot of networking. And because you're all sharing the same experiences, there is an instant and lasting bond. My best friends today are the ones I met while living overseas.

– Joanne, USAID

I went abroad when I was twenty-nine years old, and I had the time of my life!

– Kimberly, The Radiate Group

Time differences are tough to work around. The more extreme the differences, the harder it is on you. When you're single in Asia, you can end up working both day and night and almost every weekend.

– Mary, Federal Aviation Administration (FAA)

The terms "miracle worker" and "magician" are commonly used to explain our successes under extremely difficult circumstances. It is no wonder that so many of us forged lasting bonds under such intense circumstances. How could you not?

– Laura, IBM Consulting

I moved to New York from London to broaden my professional horizons and learn more about U.S. business and consumers and see the global epicenter of the pharmaceutical world from the inside. I arrived single, learned a tremendous amount, and two years later returned to London with an American fiancé. We were married a year later and now have twins.

– Kate, Edelman

As a single you may or may not be interested in dating. Depending on what country you move to, you will have a different set of challenges. Overall, though, most women who've gone before advise the same thing: If you are going single, be open to dating but be safe. Subtleties and nuances you read about or observe in the office feel very different when they are being exhibited by your partner – male or female. Everything from old wives' tales to gender stereotypes emerges when you choose to be intimate with someone from another culture. You can also try dating another expatriate or someone from your country and background who is there for the same reason. Such relationships will be forged on a common bond, but you will probably go back to your home market at some point, and then things will be different. Be warned, though: in some markets, single expat men are overwhelmed with solicitations from local women. But the same is not always true for expat women. For same sex relationships, make sure you're aware of local cultural perspectives because countries are not equally open to same sex-couples. We'll have more on dating in Chapter 5.

Making It Real

There are things about a culture that you can only learn through dating.

– Perry, coauthor and Kraft Foods, Inc.

Don't go expecting to find a boyfriend or a husband. If it happens, great. But at least in Russia, the expat men were more interested in dating the gorgeous young Russian women than someone from home. Very few expat women dated Russian men. They didn't understand us, and we thought many of them were chauvinists or alcoholics.

– Patricia, *New York Times*

I was single and 35 when I went to Singapore. The first year was very tough, but I was fortunate to find a great network of girlfriends, and we looked out for each other. In time, I met the man who would become my husband. It can happen!

– Sheila, Barclays Bank

You will be able to focus on your career, dedicating yourself to learning as much as possible without feeling the guilt of a partner and kids back home. But this could also lead to a tendency to become a workaholic overseas. There is so much to do, to learn, to accomplish. If you are in a time zone significantly ahead or behind HQ, you could easily work fourteen or more hours a day. Make sure you keep it in balance.

If You're Married

If you choose to go abroad and you are married, you will have a partner to share the ups and downs, someone to laugh with over the dumb and unavoidable cross-cultural mistakes you will make, and someone to cry with when the environment seems hostile and you want to give up. All of the married women who have moved overseas give one critical piece of advice: go only if your marriage is solid, with good communication and mutual respect, because it will be tested, stretched, and strained. With that said, living overseas will add another dimension to your relationship that you will cherish in the years to come. Your relationship will be much stronger and much more resilient because of it. Sadly, though, many marriages fail because they cannot withstand the increased strain of living abroad.

According to HR professionals and research on expatriates, a spouse's reaction and commitment to the assignment is the key reason why some expatriates are successful and some return early. This does not differ between men and women. However, the rest of the roles played by husband or wife are quite different.

First, to be a "trailing spouse," which is what the spouse of an expatriate is generally called, can be a demeaning role for anyone, but more so for a man because of gender stereotypes and expectations. In addition, it's just not as common as we would like! It can be trying to endure the social networking process of cocktail parties, neighborhood get-togethers, and office functions, especially where the only spouse who is a man may well be your husband. A man must have a great deal of self-confidence, independence, dedication, motivation, and fearlessness to be a "trailing spouse."

Second, your husband's career is an extremely important consideration because in many countries, a trailing spouse cannot legally work. If he can, it's great because he will integrate much faster. If not, nonworking spouses are faced with the task of composing a life from scratch – a challenge for which many men are not prepared. It is a brave man who agrees to face the sometimes severe social stigma of being one of the few "house husbands" in various cities around the world. Building a new life can be particularly daunting if your husband does not speak the language, does not have any friends locally, and you, in a new position, are so busy immersing yourself that you aren't much help – and possibly not even around much – in the first six months.

Third, all people moving abroad leave their network of family and friends behind. Instantly, you and your spouse become "everything" (mother, father, sister, brother, and best friend) to each other. This role can be either fulfilling or overwhelming. It may be hard to predict how your husband will react to his new role in a new culture. It is safe to assume, though, that in addition to the thrill of the newness, the first six months are going to be the most difficult for both of you – and for different reasons. You will need to devote time and effort to helping each other adjust.

Making It Real

Moving overseas with a husband as a trailing spouse can be quite difficult. The move will take its toll on both of you. It is critical that your husband feel appreciated for who he is and what he's doing for the both of you and your relationship. Be patient, kind, sensitive, appreciative, and don't focus solely on yourself and your issues at the office because he's probably experienced some highs and lows in his day as well. You may not feel they are as big or important as yours, but they are because they're his. Make sure you keep the communication open and honest and enjoy the adventure. You'll both be better off for the experience!

– **Diane, DuPont**

My husband and son were tagged to my work visa, which frequently led to questions from customs officials about my work status. My husband would genially explain that my job had taken us out of the United States. Once, he got a bit exasperated and pronounced "I'm a trailing spouse, got it?" The agent then looked at my six-year-old, who piped up with "that makes me the trailing son." International assignments that cause a formerly working spouse to stay at home can be a challenge for all egos.

— **anonymous, The New Globetrotters Survey**

My relationship with my husband was definitely strengthened by our living together overseas the first time I worked abroad. We developed a closer bond as we shared frustrating and amusing experiences together living outside the United States. By the time I moved to Russia, where I lived alone while he stayed in the U.S., I felt that we had a strong enough relationship to handle the long distance.

— **Karin, The Nature Conservancy**

Going Global With Children

Do not assume that just because you have children you shouldn't move overseas. Many women have done it and loved it. Generally, the younger the children are, the less disruptive the move will be for them. You will most likely have access to various kinds of child care, schooling, and assistance, usually offered as part of an expat package. We should note here that it will be easier if you are being transferred, as opposed to picking up and moving on your own. Most companies provide the necessary safety net for their transferred employees and this is particularly helpful with kids. Depending on what your partner is planning to do, it could be a great way for him or her to become more involved in their upbringing. There are many options for success, which depend on the country you're moving to, your company's financial assistance policy when it comes to childcare options, and the ages and health of your children.

Raising children in cross-cultural environments may be one of the most beneficial things you can ever do for them. Your adaptation, tolerance, and acceptance of things different from the norm will teach them the same. Their world will expand. They will become global citizens.

Making It Real

Going overseas to China first and then London not only helped me professionally but also allowed me to introduce my children to the big, wide wonderful world out there. They've made friends with kids from all over the world and the experiences they have had have changed them forever – for the better, I'm certain. It's wonderful to have teenagers who are already global citizens.

– Anna, former BP executive

Both of my children were born in London during my nine years there working for Reuters. They are dual citizens and have been aware of a different world view since their early years. But they are more than just international kids; they have also experienced that 'different isn't bad' in the sense that their mom, me, has worked full-time, out of the home since they were born, and their dad has been the primary caregiver, working as a freelance writer from home. It hasn't always been easy, but I believe they are so much better off for the early start on diversity and acceptance.

– Nancy, Columbia University

Going Global!

While there are serious questions you should ask yourself before embarking on an international assignment, if your gut reaction to the possibility is excitement, you should go for it. Map out your best path upward in the new global marketplace, but bear in mind that there are two accepted truths about international assignments: One is that they are never predictable – when opportunity knocks, you must answer the door! The other is that no two overseas experiences are exactly alike. But we are pretty confident that going overseas will be one of the most life-transforming and important experiences ever.

Read on about the individual tales of our six women profiled in depth in each chapter – women who, for a variety of reasons, took up the challenges of working overseas at various stages in their lives.

The Journey Continues

Perry

Growing up in a small town outside of Philadelphia, I spent more time reading *Town & Country* magazine and plotting how to become "Princess Perry" than I did thinking about becoming a global business executive. It was indeed a source of much consternation in my family when I went to college and majored in English literature and language with a minor in Russian literature and language. More than a few hours were spent around the dining table at nights between semesters discussing exactly what I was going to do to support myself upon graduation. I, with the hubris of youth, a love of learning, no understanding of the business world whatsoever, and more than my fair share of stubbornness, was not fazed by these debates. I just knew I'd find a job doing something, although I had no idea what. Thankfully, in my junior year I took a practical and infinitely helpful class called career planning and placement. After self-examination, personality tests, and group discussions, I was advised I could be just about anything I wanted. That was not much help, but in the next phase we were asked to evaluate potential careers on the basis of our lifestyle preferences and desires. This analysis provided realistic and clear options. It turned out I was most suited for a career in law or communications. With this newfound sense of purpose and a bit more research under my belt – including the realization that a career in law meant three more years of school, and I was eager to get out there and start supporting myself – I decided to go for communications. I wrote to every major company near my hometown asking them for an internship. Luckily for me, at that time the head of HR at DuPont was a fellow graduate of the University of Virginia. He decided to give me a chance, so I landed my first real professional job – in the public affairs department at DuPont's worldwide headquarters in Wilmington. It was 1985. I hadn't even turned twenty-one. I knew nothing. I was placed in a big vacant office next to a kind and impressive man who was the head of international public affairs at the time. This experience turned out to be pivotal in my career and my life. First of all, it taught me how much I didn't know. Second, it taught me that the pace of promotion in big corporations in the 1980s wasn't for me. Third, it enabled me to begin building a network of contacts. Finally, it was a key factor in my getting a great job after graduation at a local communications agency that had DuPont as one of its major clients.

Two moves later, I was headed for Singapore. I was twenty-five years old, with four years of professional experience. I was a single girl from a small town. I knew only two things about Singapore: it was hot year-round and, at 5'8", I thought I might actually be one of the tallest women in the country. But I am so glad I had the nerve to get on the plane!

Patricia

I had a passion for history and languages and became fascinated by Russia after taking a history course in college on the Russian Revolution – so fascinated that after graduation, when I was living in the woods in Vermont, I started taking Russian language through correspondence courses. After milking the cows and feeding the pigs, I would sit by the wood stove and try to decipher the strange alphabet and grammar. Then I had a chance to spend a month studying in Russia and fell in love with the country. Later, I received a scholarship to Columbia's School of International Affairs, and, thinking I'd probably work at the U.S. State Department one day, I focused on Soviet Affairs. I had the opportunity, however, to take a few courses at their well-respected Columbia Graduate School of Journalism. I did so and discovered that journalism was my calling. When I finished my masters, I was offered and took a job in Washington, D.C., at McGraw-Hill, which owns *BusinessWeek*. By this time, I knew I wanted to be a foreign correspondent, and I was determined to make it happen. It was difficult to land a foreign correspondent's job, and I specifically wanted to work in Russia. I kept trying to work overseas, but to no avail.

Finally, opportunity came in the form of a layoff. McGraw-Hill closed the unit I worked for, and I received a handsome payout for my years of service. I decided to take the money, take a chance, and move to Russia. I had been studying Russian with a private tutor, who assured me she could get me a private visa (visas were extremely difficult to get in the early 1990s). She delivered. I moved to Russia with a good command of the Russian language, professional journalism credentials, some money in my pocket, a bit of luck, and no job. I was thirty-five and single but had left

48

my long-standing boyfriend back in Washington, D.C., committed to doing the best I could to maintain the relationship long distance. It wasn't
easy, considering the time differences, the lack of good telephone service,
and no e-mail. He chose not to move with me because he didn't have the
same passion for Russia that I did and did not want to give up a job at
home that he loved. Besides, Moscow was pretty grim in 1990. We both
also worried that I wouldn't make enough money as a freelancer to support two of us. But I wanted to take a chance and see what I could do. I
gave myself three months to make it work, and if not, I would return to
the U.S. and look for a job. It worked.

Jackie

I'm not exactly sure when it happened, but it was early on in my life,
probably when I was thirteen or fourteen years old. In fact, on a recent
trip to see my parents, my mother showed me a journal from my youth
containing my hopes for the future: At the top of the list were working
for a large company and living in a French-speaking country. I remember
writing it, and though I must have been thinking ahead about what I
wanted to do with my life, I'm not sure I ever really imagined that life
could be as interesting as mine has been up to now. I had started taking
French at that age and then went on a class trip to France at the age of
sixteen. I loved the language and the travel, and had an inspirational
teacher who encouraged all of us to learn about other people and cultures
to broaden our horizons.

I graduated from the University of Texas at Arlington with under-
graduate and graduate degrees in economics and went to work for LTV
Aerospace and Defense, followed by Celanese Chemical Company, and
then switched to Alcon as a financial analyst. For the next seven years, I
enjoyed rapid promotions and the opportunity to work across a broad
spectrum of finance, including planning and reporting, controlling, and
treasury. I was lucky enough to be able to get involved in various projects
that had international components, so I was never quite far away from the
global work, which I enjoyed. This opportunity was due in part to the fact
that I worked for an international company and also because I displayed
an aptitude for grasping the intricacies of international issues versus purely

domestic ones. Once I was on these projects, I was able to demonstrate another skill: managing relationships. I had good success working with non-Americans and thus continued to get the international assignments.

I had about ten years of experience and a fairly diverse background for a finance person when I was asked to go work in the global headquarters for Nestlé in Vevey, Switzerland. I was single, thirty-two years old, and I couldn't wait to go – my dream was about to come true. I received a significant promotion to Assistant Controller for the Pharma-Cosmetics Group, responsible for coordinating all of Alcon's financial and operating relationships with Nestlé. I was to be the resident Alcon representative while working for Nestlé, a truly international company. I was a little apprehensive of the "unknown" of moving overseas, but I instinctively knew that it was a super opportunity that shouldn't be passed up. I knew some business colleagues in Switzerland, and Western Europe had a lifestyle similar enough for me that I didn't feel too much adaptation was required. Mostly, I was excited about the opportunity to live and work in Switzerland, and I knew that if I didn't like it, I could always come back home or go somewhere else.

Stacie

I grew up traveling and loved the thrill of it, the newness and adventure – especially overseas. In college, my close circle of friends were not American, including my (still) best friend (and godmother to my daughters), Eleonora, from Rome; Richard and Frederic from Paris; and Rachid, from Morocco. I found that I felt much more comfortable with them than with other American students. After receiving my degree in communication theory and completing graduate coursework in English literature at Florida Atlantic University, I moved to Washington, D.C., and hoped to get a job with an international company. Burson-Marsteller – at the time the largest and most prestigious public relations firm in the world – hired me. During my first few years, I did my best to impress on them my international aspirations. Anytime I was planning an international excursion or "going along for the ride" with a friend or family member who had business overseas (i.e., if I could find a cheap air ticket, hotel would be covered), I made the most of it by doing two critical things: One, I let my boss know where I was going and emphasized that I wanted to work internationally one day; and two, I asked if she could introduce me to someone in a B-M office in that particular city. I met so many interesting people, visited offices around the world, participated in a few brainstorming sessions for clients, and, above all, created a reputation for myself as someone who wanted to do business internationally – so much so that I was willing to take time on my personal vacations to meet work colleagues.

I was twenty-nine years old when I moved to Hong Kong. I was a middle manager and had six years of experience. I was fortunate to have two great mentors who worked with management to fast-track my career and better prepare me for my next move. My husband, Mike, and I got married one the eve of our departure. We stopped for a two-week honeymoon in India (who would pass up the opportunity to visit the Taj Mahal on your honeymoon?). Mike was thrilled at the opportunity to live in Asia and extremely supportive. Although it was risky going international so early in our marriage, the pay-off was big: we built lasting, special bonds. Mike knew first-hand the benefits of overseas experience, as he had lived in Stockholm and was currently working at an environmental think tank that focused on developing markets. He was willing to leave his job to accompany me, but he did have one request: that we travel and explore the region – not work all the time. We took extended weekend jaunts to beach locales, added on a few days to my professional trips to tour all the major cities in the region, and planned three-week-long vacations to immerse ourselves in various cultures. Our three years were so much richer because of it. Mike worked in Hong Kong, but he had to reinvent himself. He turned his research and writing skills into a new profession as a freelance photojournalist specializing in travel and history. He wrote for the *South China Morning Post*, Hong Kng's most respected English-language newspaper, as well as for several magazines in the region. As he became more well-known, he began contributing stories to newspapers in the United States, building a network that he put to use upon his return. He continues this profession today.

Diane

I left the University of Notre Dame with a degree in chemical engineering. I chose DuPont over other multinational companies because it had a reputation for its versatile environment where one could grow and expand. Starting out in the laboratory, next I moved on to customer service, which I loved, and then asked to move to sales. I thrived on the freedom, the flexibility, and the challenges. During this time, I met my husband, Ed, who lived in Washington, D.C. We got married, and although Ed had to give up his established carpentry business, he moved to Chicago to be with me and start his business anew. After five years and five bosses in Chicago, I knew that I needed to get to know the right players in Wilmington, DuPont's HQ. I had a great mentor, who encouraged me to return to HQ, where I got a big promotion to lead a team of 20 design engineers specifically for customer design support. Gaining management experience and now back in front of senior leadership, my next move was to go overseas. At the time of my first transfer, I was thirty-two years old and thrilled to be moving for my long-awaited first international assignment. With ten years in several functions to my credit, I was ready personally and professionally. I received a significant promotion to European business manager for engineering polymers, a pan-European high-profile job running a $250 million P&L, based in Geneva, Switzerland. As he was in the two previous moves, Ed was supportive, excited, and ready to go. Despite my communicating this point to HR, they insisted that we have a meeting as a couple to review tax-related and other financial information. In that meeting, they questioned Ed and asked him if he really wanted to go. They repeated several times that he could not work in Switzerland. They had a hard time believing that he wanted to go and wouldn't try to work despite the local laws. Ed wanted to go and viewed this opportunity as his "get out of jail free" card – a time not to work but to enjoy life. He was thrilled and extremely supportive. Though he would be a trailing spouse, neither one of us wanted him to live in my professional shadow. Ed was determined to develop his own identity and program, which he did. After more than four years in Europe, he learned to speak French, German, and Dutch; he skied some of the most difficult terrain in Europe; and he improved his golf handicap from 24 to 5. I couldn't have been as successful without him there by my side sharing in the adventure.

Anna

I secured an internship with Amoco after my freshman year in college. Following that first summer, I was signed on as an employee with an extended absence for three years while I finished school. I interned every summer and got a big boost in professional experience this way. I met my husband, Joel, in college and we were married a year after I graduated from the University of Illinois with a degree in marketing and business administration. At the time, I knew Amoco was a great company, but I had no idea that I would have the opportunity to play such a significant international role for it in my parents' homeland. I am Chinese American and grew up speaking Mandarin. I had always considered myself lucky to be bilingual and hoped to be able to work in China one day.

I began my career as a territory manager in Grand Forks, North Dakota, which at the time seemed halfway to the North Pole. I was blessed early on in my career with a series of rapid promotions and broad experience in sales, marketing, and customer service across the Midwestern part of the United States. One of the secrets to my success is my husband, Joel. He supported me 100 percent through my career choices. We have always approached decisions as choices that were best for us, the family — not just one of us. We had our first child nine and a half years after we were married — always waiting for the "right time" to have a baby, hoping our jobs would slow down, but it never happened! I was pregnant with our second child when the opportunity to go to China arose. I was thirty-five years old and director, products research and development, with about 100 people reporting to me. I was ready for the challenge.

So was Joel. Although he had never lived outside Illinois, Joel agreed and saw it as an opportunity to learn about me: my background, culture, and language — as well as to better understand the 50 percent cultural makeup of his children. Joel didn't work in China, but he adapted quite well, setting his own objectives. He enrolled in the Beijing Language Institute, immersed himself in the culture, and, as often as he could, he wandered through the shops and local neighborhoods, exploring and trying to practice his Mandarin. When we left two years later, he had achieved his goal of becoming conversationally fluent – not an easy feat.

Joel also oversaw the household. Our children were two and a half years old and three months old when we moved, and we hired a wonderful nanny – one who spoke only Mandarin. Our kids were well cared for and adapted quite well. But because of their young ages, we felt that adequate health care and medical attention were imperative to our going. Before we moved, I made sure the facilities on the ground were satisfactory, and, as a backup, we maintained regular contact with our doctor back in Chicago just in case we needed additional advice or a second opinion – even if it was over the telephone. This, our first foray into international waters, created lasting family bonds and set the stage for future international adventures.

Chapter 3

Landing an
International Assignment

**You can't tell enough people, often enough, about your desire
to go overseas.**
— Diane, DuPont

Landing your first international assignment is typically the hardest part of
launching your global career. Once you've decided that working overseas
is right for you, you need a plan to make it happen. Given the competi-
tiveness of the global job market today, securing an international assignment is not necessarily easy. However, if you have a combination of top-
notch professional skills (or the equivalent in academic terms), perseverance, and some plain old-fashioned good luck, you can do it.

There are, of course, many things you can do to increase your chances
of "getting lucky." You can show up at more meetings, raise your hand
for more assignments, make contacts with international leaders, and network. And of course, be willing to give 100 percent all the time, even if it
means long hours and sacrificed weekends.

Making It Real

I was lucky that my Russian tutor had such great connections in
Moscow. She helped me get a visa, which was extremely difficult
in 1990 — especially for journalists.

— Patricia, *New York Times*

If I hadn't been in the personnel meeting (I was filling in for my
boss) that day to hear about the opportunity in Europe, I wonder
if I would have ever gone international.

— Diane, DuPont

Whether you target an expat position within your existing company, choose to switch jobs because of an international posting, or plan to move abroad with some skills and contacts but no job, you need to be clear about your objective, your strategy, and your action plan. While it is important to be open to opportunities that simply present themselves (which is the way many women went abroad for the first time), we suggest a three-step approach to sort through the various factors and streamline your thinking.

Step 1: Defining your objective(s): What do you want to achieve?
Step 2: Devising a strategy to get you there: What are the best ways to achieve your objective?
        Gathering intelligence
        Networking
        Picking the best market for you
Step 3: Marketing yourself: How do you plan to package the information and sell yourself?

Step 1: Defining Your Objective(s)

As the proverb says, if you don't know where you are heading, any road will get you there. Your first step in the planning process, therefore, is to determine exactly what your objective is – if you have more than one, prioritize. Although some people know exactly why they want to work abroad, many don't. Some of the most common reasons the women we surveyed went overseas are as follows:

- Excitement and travel
- Drawn to a particular part of the world
- To get ahead faster than my peers
- To learn new and different skills
- Faster financial rewards
- Ability to make a difference in others' lives

For most of us, it is a mixture of these factors.

Step 2: Devising a Strategy to Get You There

Once you have established your objective(s), develop an action plan designed to reach your goal. Our approach to devising the best strategy for you includes a three-part process. First, gather intelligence through fact-finding. Second, network and build your international contacts. Third, consider the pros and cons of various regions, countries, and cultures. Although luck and/or happenstance can lead you on a particular journey, doing your research upfront will enable you to better understand your options, carry on potentially productive conversations with colleagues and co-workers, and make more informed choices. Your research should include determining what type of organization you'd like to work for (e.g., corporate vs. nonprofit, large vs. midsize; which regions, countries, and cultures you're interested in and those you would rule out; and what value you would bring to an overseas posting (e.g., language skills, cultural familiarity, or a specific business skill).

Gathering Intelligence

- **Monitor business trends.** Investigate business issues, problems, consumers, and clients within your industry at home and outside your market. Ask leaders within your organization what trends or business opportunities they believe might be just around the corner in other countries or regions, and why. For example, the growing middle classes of China and India mean more consumers, and more consumers mean more marketing and sales of consumer products and services. Attend lectures and seminars at universities, nongovernmental organizations (NGOs), or business conferences to hear what the experts are saying about what the future might hold.

- **Pay attention to world events**. Watch, listen to, and read international news. Bone up on your history, geography, and political science. Begin to learn a relevant language, such as Mandarin, Arabic, or Spanish. Pay attention to coming events, such as where the next Summer Olympics will be (Brazil 2016), as a great deal of growth and activity takes place in the years immediately preceding. Sometimes countries with existing tensions have rebirths and booms after the turmoil has subsided, as occurred in Vietnam or Eastern Europe. The fall of the Berlin wall created a huge interest in the "East German" market almost overnight. It's a gamble, but those on the ground first tend to benefit the most.

- **Surf the web.** Thanks to the Internet, so much more information can be shared across borders. Check out the web sites for such international organizations as the U.S. Chamber of Commerce, the U.S. State Department, the United Nations, the World Bank, and international think tanks such as the Brookings Institute. Most provide lots of information on working and living abroad.

- **Find out who the international players are.** If you don't work for a global organization, find out which companies and organizations are global. You'll discover that many claim to be global but really aren't, having only token offices or a shoestring network. Unless you're looking at the Fortune 500 list of global companies (which is a terrific resource, as are the individual lists by region), you'll have to sift through annual reports examining business strategies, international diversity at the senior management level, and revenue distribution throughout various regions to get a good idea of how international they really are. Web sites can also indicate global sophistication if they address consumers in multiple languages and highlight case studies, consumers, and products from around the world. You can also use search engines to track organizations and various countries to determine their level of activity as reported by the media. If you work for an international organization, find out where it has offices, affiliates, and partners. Learn about the various international projects, and try to work on one. In addition to beginning to get a feel for the market, you'll learn what you like and don't like – both are equally important when it comes to a making a decision about moving to another country. In addition, you'll begin to meet some players outside your home turf.

- **Follow your heart.** If there is a part of the world where you feel passionate about making a difference, research international NGOs, such as The Jane Goodall Institute to help save wild chimpanzees and the rain forests in Africa, or international foundations, such as the Bill and Melinda Gates Foundation to help educate people throughout the developing world on preventative measures regarding HIV/AIDS and malaria. Most countries have not-for-profit foreign aid organizations that operate beyond their borders. Many of these organizations hire internationally inclined professionals in order to execute their programs around the world.

After careful consideration of the information you have gleaned, take a hard look at what you can do that's different or that would bring value to your company or another organization. Package your thinking so that when you begin the networking process, you have something meaningful to say.

A Few Words About the U.S. Peace Corps

In 1961, the United States set up the Peace Corps, a federal government agency devoted to world peace and friendship. Since then, some 182,000 volunteers have served in 138 countries. They've been teachers and mentors to children. They've helped farmers grow crops, worked with small businesses to market products, and shown women how to care for their babies. They've helped students develop computer skills and educated communities about the threat of HIV/AIDS. The Peace Corps prides itself on its ability to adapt and respond to current issues, and the volunteers meet challenges with a spirit of dedication and resourcefulness.

If you are an American citizen, the Peace Corps is an excellent way to begin your international career, and current programs even combine graduate degrees with your assignment so you don't have to choose one or the other. Many former volunteers have leveraged the skills and experiences they gained overseas to build professions across all sectors. Like other people who have gained international experience, Peace Corps volunteers have gained a great deal of confidence, independent judgment, and cross-cultural resourcefulness recognized by all employers in all professions.

Source: www.PeaceCorps.gov

Making It Real

I joined the Peace Corps and was sent to Botswana. I helped establish a secondary school and oversaw the teaching staff. I got two and a half years of real business experience straight out of college. I loved living in Africa so much that I moved to Malawi to work for a hotel group, where I developed a training curriculum for its employees and actually trained them. I then started my own business – a cooperative of eight local tailors – that I then sold before I went back to the United States. To all recent graduates who want to work internationally right out of school, the Peace Corps is a great way to do it.

– Jeanne, human resource training consultant

Networking

The importance of networking cannot be overstated. Relationships remain critical in most places around the world. Who you know is just as important as what you know – and it certainly increases your chances of "getting lucky," as you are more likely to hear about possible opportunities or be at the top of someone's mind when positions arise if you are well-known among those in the know. Building your international network is a critical step to your success before, during, and after your international assignment. Doing so, however, can be tough, especially if you have limited international business experience. Networking is all about a mutually beneficial exchange with another who has something that might prove useful one day. So how do you get started?

- **Ask for contacts from anyone and everyone.** HR, supervisors, executive search firms, book clubs, alumni associations, neighbors, friends, and family all probably know a few people who have worked or are working abroad. Ask for informational interviews so that you can get to know these globetrotters. Get their advice, and request contacts and door-openers to further expand your contact list. Most expats enjoy talking about their experiences and want to share their insights with interested listeners. In addition, expats tend to stay interconnected much longer than other work relationships. Tapping into their personal network can be quite beneficial.

Making It Real

I networked internally at Citibank, getting to know as many people internationally as possible. When I was transferred to another position, I let this new supervisor know that I was interested in working abroad. Within one year, he offered me the opportunity to work in Singapore, where I worked for five years. From there

I went to London for Barclays, a much easier move because I'd already become an international professional.

– Sheila, Barclays Bank

- **Make your intentions known.** Be sure to let your immediate supervisors know of your objectives and do your best to them on board. You will need their support and recommendation if you are put up for a position.

- **Get to know the international players within your own organization.** If you work for an international organization and/or one with overseas affiliates, find out who the regional leaders and global managers are, how they got there (if not a local national), and whatever personal information about them you can learn. If a meeting is being held that will be attended by global leadership – those living elsewhere – schedule a meeting so you can convey your desire to go to their region, country, or business unit. Spark their interest with a perspective about the value you might bring to their country or business unit, or an opportunity for growth that you think might be relevant to pursue. Most of these individuals will take the time to meet with a colleague, and if they believe you have a genuine interest and something substantive to offer, they'll help you.

- **Volunteer for a global project.** The fastest way to build your network internally is to work on a global project. You can build relationships through common work product, conference calls, and if you're lucky, a visit to the overseas site. You can also use this experience to build relationships with the local organization by helping the people there succeed.

- **Use personal travel.** Whether as a means to target and establish local contacts or offer assistance to local offices/affiliates to demonstrate to your boss your love of travel and spirit of adventure, personal international travel can be immensely productive. When you travel to another country as a tourist, set up meetings with those on your growing contact list, and/or cold-call companies in your industry (see "Get to know the international players" above).

Making It Real

I went on holiday to Eastern Europe, as I had become personally fascinated with the region after the fall of the Berlin Wall. While I was preparing for the trip, a friend put me in touch with her colleague, an American woman living and working in Prague. Upon arrival, I contacted the colleague, who in turn introduced me to a number of other expatriates based there. After returning to Los Angeles and my job, I maintained loose contact with my new Prague friends. A few months later, I received a call from one of them about a great job opportunity. I had always had international ambitions, but in a conversation a year or two earlier with my employer, the LA office of a global advertising agency, I was told that the plum jobs – in London, Paris, or Milan – were reserved for senior agency executives. I had not given any thought to emerging markets. I agreed to the interview, knowing that I would have to fly at my own expense. This was a significant cost, so I needed to justify it to myself. I began building a list of all the ad agencies, MNCs (multinational corporations), and media corporations that had a presence in Eastern Europe. I cold-called them prior to my visit and managed to secure a significant number of back-to-back interviews. One meeting in Vienna turned into an opportunity to work for Ogilvy & Mather in Moscow. I was granted a Russian visa and within twenty-four hours was interviewing for the job in Moscow. I accepted weeks later and moved from Los Angeles to Moscow just six months after I'd returned from vacation.

– Kimberly, The Radiate Group

- **Find a mentor.** Someone with international experience can help open doors, make calls, and guide you as you explore this fascinating life outside your home country. You can find such leaders within your current organization, possibly through your university, via an international organization, or through friends.

One last noteworthy point about networking is that this book would have been impossible to write without the combined network both of us have built over the years. The hundreds of women who participated in our survey and contributed quotes and anecdotes providing insight and advice throughout this book are invaluable to us.

Being Market Savvy

You will begin to develop a sense of places, organizations, people, and experiences overseas – and an emerging strategy for achieving your objective. Now it's time to think specifically about various markets. Keep in mind that you may not be able to pick your market; you may have to accept what's offered. Some women we surveyed had a particular desire to go to a specific country or region and made it happen. Others spoke a particular language, which narrowed their choices, but made the integration process that much easier. Still others went where they were offered a job.

To choose a market, you must compare the opportunity with the specifics and drawbacks of that market. We've pulled together a list of salient points to consider when evaluating whether or not you should consider, accept, or decline an offer or opportunity to live abroad. The first three points are considered the most important by the majority of women we surveyed.

Tips on How to Pick a Market

1. **Business needs.** If you're most interested in getting ahead in your organization, go where they need you to go. It will give you the best chance of negotiating a good deal, ensure you're viewed as a team player, and, assuming you succeed, help you become a real corporate asset.

Making It Real

I had not planned on leaving Singapore, but when the call came asking me to move to Russia, I knew it was important to the firm. I didn't particularly want to go to Moscow – especially not on Christmas Eve – but I knew that if I did, the firm would recognize my willingness to help out, which in turn would create a bank of goodwill that I could call on down the road. So I traded in my two-piece bathing suit for a pair of ice skates and moved from Singapore to Moscow.

– Perry, coauthor and Kraft Foods, Inc.

I went to China at thirty. I was working for a management consulting firm in a niche market entry and the only non-China expert on the team. On a business trip, I took some time to travel around, fell in love with the experience, and decided this was the place for me. It wasn't the country or culture so much as the buzz in the air – it was similar to that in Silicon Valley in the early 90s, but multiplied a few times. If this same buzz existed in another country, I believe I would be just as happy there.

– Angie, Hudson Recruitment

2. **Personal interest**. Although most women we spoke with agree that you must have some interest in the country and its culture, language, or customs, it needn't be your number-one choice. As long as you are interested and find the country appealing, you can do well.

3. **Safety, Culture, Environment, and Health.** Certain things are critical to your personal quality of life. If any of these important qualities are significantly compromised, you may not be able to meet your potential, and you probably won't do a good job. Your discomfort could cut short your stay, which can have a negative effect on future postings. The most important elements of comfort are your (and your family's, if applicable) personal well-being, ability to integrate, and religion. For example, many big cities are polluted and thus not great for small children. Likewise, if you or a family member has a medical condition that requires close supervision or quick access to high-quality health care, you will want to steer clear of less developed countries. Some countries are less accepting of single women or those in same-sex relationships, so you'll want to be sure your personal status is accepted and won't cause unmanageable discomfort once you are on the ground. If religion is important to you, find out how your religion is accepted in the area you are considering going to.

4. **Cost of living.** If you are being transferred, you'll need a package that you and your organization deem to be fair. If moving on your own, you'll need to be sure you can survive on local currency, though you should have some reserves for the unexpected. Also, be sure to anticipate a margin of error. If you feel too financially strapped, you probably will not be able to perform. Don't underestimate the importance of feeling financially secure – with everything else you'll be taking on, worrying about making the rent each month could put you over the edge.

5. **Language skills.** There is no real consensus over the importance of possessing language skills of the country to which you're going. The key is this: what value do you bring? If you have excellent technical skills, management experience, or in-depth knowledge of your company, for example, your professional contributions may outweigh the need for local language skills. If not, then you need to learn quickly. If the market you are going to accommodates English-speakers – like most of Europe and Asia – you should still learn to speak the local language (at a conversational level at least), as it will help you integrate faster. Also, you are more likely to pick up subtle nuances or tidbits that you would otherwise miss. Making the effort to learn the language while you're on the ground earns you "big points," as it attests to your personal commitment to that culture. Finally, if you are based in a market that does not use your first language as its first language, chances are that most important transactions will be done through translators, so, at a minimum, you can get by.

Making It Real

Learn the language (even if you begin after you arrive). I didn't speak any Russian when I landed, but five years later I was teaching international accounting standards at Moscow State University in Russian. Not only will learning the language help you to be more quickly accepted by the locals, it will also open up an entire world outside the expat-social group.

– Pamela, The Teagarden Group

6. **Up-and-coming hot spots.** There will always be markets and industries on the rise. Those who can anticipate where and when these hot spots will materialize can capitalize enormously. For example, places like China, India, South Africa, Brazil, Mexico, and the Middle East are currently on the radar screens of most organizations, and there is a boom in business, sales, and often, hiring. However, many, but not all, are "developing" markets, and you must appreciate the difference.

Making It Real

Some markets, such as the United States and Switzerland, are "black and white" with fifty-page contracts and strict rules for engagement. Others, such as China, are "gray" with deals done over dinner and a handshake. Hot spots carry high risk and high reward because they are usually unfamiliar territory.

– Anna, former BP executive

7. **Familiarity.** If you have spent any time in a country and/or have colleagues, friends, or family living there, you'll experience less culture shock and therefore will probably be able to hit the ground running.

8. **Heritage.** Some people choose a country on the basis of their family background. This is strictly personal consideration and either matters or doesn't. You decide.

9. **Regional or national.** Depending on your industry, level, and career plans, you may decide that going to one large country, such as China, would be more advantageous than going to a smaller country that operates within a region, such as Switzerland. A larger market will allow you to focus on that country and culture, its consumer, and its overall economic and political specifics. You are more likely to become a country expert this way. By going to a smaller country, you will have broader access and learning across the region, which has its business benefits as well. One specific benefit is leveraging this regional role into another regional role in another part of the world to gain greater global experience.

Making It Real

I chose Hong Kong because it was the regional HQ for so many MNCs, as well as the gateway to China. I knew I'd be able to work not only in one of the most fascinating cities in the world, but across a region rich with history, culture, language, and diversity. The experience broadened my horizons so much more than a one-country position would have, and it added an entire region to my resume.

– Stacie, coauthor and consultant

10. **Family factor.** Depending on whether you are single or married, have children or not, you will need to weigh the pros and cons of your personal situation vis-à-vis various markets. For example, some may not allow your spouse to work, though he may want to. Do your homework and assess the facts against your specific needs.

Working in the United States should not be underestimated for most nationalities. Having professional experience in the United States could turn out to be essential on your path to global leadership of a large multinational company or organization. However, transferring to the United States may not be as easy as it seems. According to Stephen McGarry, WPP's director of global mobility, New York is probably the most difficult destination for employees on international assignments: "Even though the city has a constant influx of new residents, it can be a hard place to adapt, particularly because of the housing market. There are so many neighborhoods, so many pockets of diversity, and real estate moves at lightning speed – despite the high prices. Employees on assignment can feel overwhelmed at their options…and are exposed to the reality of the city: You need to come with your checkbook in hand, and, even if you have the funds to be able to afford the apartment, without a U.S. Social Security number and a credit history in the United States, there is a good chance you will not get it."

As part of your exploration into various countries, be sure to check out cultural stereotypes related to ethnicity, religion, and gender. Being honest with yourself about who you are and what other countries are like is critical to your success. Some countries have practices that you may not be able to abide. Some may have gender-specific roles that you will not be comfortable with. Appreciate the fact that there are countries and cultures where you will never be truly accepted. Conversely, don't rule out every market just because there are some things you don't like.

Step 3: Marketing Yourself

After you've done your homework, you need to begin marketing yourself internally and externally. Companies spend a significant amount of money in relocating employees abroad, so they want to be sure that you have not only the desire and the skills, but also the character traits necessary to succeed. In addition to positioning yourself in a manner that illustrates how you could add value to your company in a particular country, you should highlight those character traits commonly accepted as critical to an expatriate, as detailed in Chapter One. Collect recent examples of your adaptability and flexibility, ability to communicate well, patience and persistence, curiosity and open-mindedness, and skill at building teams and relationships. These examples will prove invaluable when you are being assessed as a potential candidate for an overseas position. Be the person who always finds a way to make things happen. Continue to perform well, and take on interesting international assignments if you can. By now, you should have a good idea of what to do to land a position overseas. In the meantime, here are some pointers from women who've done it.

Ten Ways to Increasing Your Chances of Going Global

1. Perform your current duties with excellence.
2. Make your international desires known often and broadly. Incorporate talk of an international assignment into your formal performance reviews.
3. Find a mentor to advocate for you, especially one with an international network.
4. Learn and/or practice a foreign language.
5. Research those countries you might be transferred to so that you can make an informed decision.
6. Demonstrate your cultural awareness and sensitivity while still in your home market.
7. Point out ways you can make a difference for your organization overseas.
8. Package yourself and your accomplishments in a non-self-serving way that demonstrates your potential value.
9. Volunteer for special projects involving international work.
10. If you believe that you will not be transferred by an organization, you can move to the country of your choice on your own.

Making It Real

Prove your value to the organization in your own country first. Like the stock market, organizations want "predictability" in their employees; they want to be confident there will be a good return on their investment if they spend the money and take the risk in sending you overseas.

– Joanne, USAID

As the head of global HR, whenever someone asks me how to get considered for an international assignment, I advise them to do a few things. First, identify a market and take a vacation there to see if you really like it as much as you think. Two, find out about work you have in common with that office. Look for things you could even work on from your current home base – when you finally arrive, you'll be able to make an impact right away. Third, discuss the idea with your family, and surface any objections well in advance of details being discussed.

– Celia, Burson-Marsteller

One last point. Although planning is critical, flexibility is perhaps even more important. Our research has found that many people began international careers with one plan, only to end up in completely different positions as they learned about themselves and progressed in their lives and careers. You never know where the path will lead, but in the end, that's one of the best things about working internationally: It opens up *lots* of doors. It's up to you to decide which ones you go through.

Read on about the various paths each of our six successful internationalists took. Not only is there no single formula for landing that big overseas assignment, but many things can happen on your way abroad, including the arrival of Lady Luck in the nick of time.

The Journey Continues

Stacie

During my first few years at Burson-Marsteller, I worked with a variety of clients with many different issues to build as broad a skill set as possible. I had two excellent mentors who were senior leaders in the agency and who worked closely with me, teaching me core skills to fill up my tactical tool box. Their constant direction and oversight in a fast-paced, demanding, client-centered business created an intense training ground, one in which I was stretched intellectually through demanding client assignments. This high-growth period in the junior stage of my career yielded an advanced approach to client problem solving, which involved three critical skills: keen perception of both verbal and nonverbal clues, thinking critically about all aspects of a problem in order to get to the heart of it and therefore the right solution, and building relationships – up, down, and across. These skills have stayed with me and served me well.

Despite being somewhat junior, I was tapped to work with senior leaders and therefore was able to work on some of B-M's exciting international accounts. In a short time, I proved I could work successfully and diplomatically with senior members of foreign governments and leading businessmen and -women of other nationalities. More importantly, I proved I could grasp multiple sides of a story in order to develop a win-win solution for all. When an opportunity to work in the firm's Indian affiliate arose, I volunteered for it, which caught the eye of many senior leaders, including the CEO. Although the Indian assignment never materialized, this got the ball rolling for me to be interviewed for assignments in Buenos Aires, Tokyo, Hong Kong, and Singapore. A good friend and colleague had recently moved to Singapore, and she recommended that I move to Asia, as it was "where the action was" – it was the mid-1990s. She loved it, was performing extremely well, and had thus paved the way for other like-minded women interested in the challenge of Asia.

For me, it was great to have options. After numerous discussions with regional leaders in Latin America and Asia-Pacific, conducting my own research on the fastest growing markets, and discussions with my fiancée, I opted for Hong Kong. I believed that I could probably have the greatest impact there – a largely English-speaking city that was undergoing significant political and economic change. And so, the day after our wedding, we began our married life as a couple of expats in one of the most exciting cities in the world, Hong Kong.

Diane

Throughout my first ten years at DuPont, I had always made it known to HR, my supervisors, and anyone who would listen that I wanted an international assignment. Every year, during my personnel review, I made sure my desire to work overseas was noted. Working hard and performing well, I developed a solid track record of delivering new business and customer sales that spoke for itself. I was a quick study and had good interpersonal skills, packaging myself as a great middle manager who would succeed in most any job. So, when an opening for a European position

70

was announced in a personnel meeting one day, I hoped that I would be nominated. However, as capable men's names were being tossed around, I realized that if I didn't speak up for myself, no one else would. So, on a break, I mustered my courage and asked the boss of my boss's boss for the job. He was quite taken aback and questioned my sincerity. I was questioned whether or not I knew what I was doing, i.e., did my husband know of my requests. I assured them I did; they should leave the personal details to me, for I wanted the job. Lady Luck shined on me that day: my name would not have been brought up by anyone else, despite my years of expressed desire to work overseas, if I hadn't spoken up for myself.

About three weeks after the meeting, I got a call from my boss, who offered me the position. I knew I could do this job – one that focused on customers, my favorite part of the business and one I excelled in – but it would be a new challenge taking these skills and applying them across multiple countries in one large region. I was about to take on responsibility for $250 million worth of business across multiple currencies, languages, cultures, and customs. I would have people reporting to me with whom I did not share a common first language. I would be one of the few women leaders, certainly one of the few American women. I was blazing a trail, and, yes, I was a little scared, but I was up for it. I knew that if I listened to others, asked good questions, and built a good team where everyone could do their best work and be rewarded for it, I would be fine. I believe that great leaders are great learners. I left for Switzerland knowing there was a lot to learn.

Perry

In 1988, I was working for a local public relations firm in Wilmington, Delaware. I liked it, but I wanted to go overseas. I knew that would never be possible with a local firm. So, I researched and wrote to all of the major international PR firms, offering a deal: I would work for them in any city in the United States for two years. In return, if I was successful, they would send me overseas. At the time, "overseas" meant "Europe" to me. Within a month, I got lucky – a firm responded favorably to my idea. Soon thereafter I was off to Baltimore. Each quarter during my two years there, I wrote to the North American CEO, telling him about what I was doing for the firm and reminding him of our "deal." At the end of those two years, I had indeed proved myself and been successful, so I pushed for the promised overseas post. The Berlin Wall had recently fallen, and I was thinking Germany. But when the call came, it was not Germany or anywhere else in Europe. It was Singapore. I knew little of Singapore, and what I knew did not sound appealing, so I indicated I was not that interested and was really hoping for Europe. A few days later I got a follow-up call. It was the CEO, saying I should just talk with the woman leading the project they wanted me to work on in Singapore, as she was great and I was sure to like her. I talked with her. Indeed she was great. But it was still Singapore. I had a boyfriend. I had a home. A car. Good friends. Singapore seemed far away from all of that. By the third call, I also knew that if I didn't take this offer, there wouldn't be another one for a very long time. I went for it, thinking: what's the worst thing that could happen? I could hate it, but if I did, I knew I could just come home. In the end, I didn't hate it, in fact, I loved being overseas so much I lived abroad for nearly ten years.

Jackie

I was recognized as an "HP," a high-potential employee, in Alcon, which had been good to me by moving me into different positions early in my career. Thanks to a combination of the great opportunities offered and my ability to consistently meet and sometimes exceed expectations on different and difficult assignments, I was getting noticed by senior management. Personally, I loved the challenge and consistently volunteered to work on all kinds of projects to enhance my financial skills, as well as prove that I could go the extra mile. I knew that great financial skills were important, but so was my ability to differentiate myself from my peers. As a result of working on these projects, many of which were international in nature, a few important things took place. One, I broadened my financial skills across multiple disciplines within finance (e.g., controlling, treasury, planning, reporting) in a short time. Two, I practiced and honed my managerial and interpersonal skills, eventually achieving a maturity level beyond my years of experience. Three, I worked with, and got to know, many colleagues in other parts of the world, including those in Nestlé,

Alcon's parent company, and was able to demonstrate my proficiency in several languages.

When the opportunity arose to work for Alcon in Switzerland, I was manager of corporate investments. I was approached by my boss, who had spoken with senior management. They all thought the opportunity would be a good one for me and Alcon: I would represent Alcon well within the Nestlé conglomerate, and I would learn about Nestlé and eventually bring back key learnings. In addition, because I spoke French, I could hit the ground running. I looked at the opportunity as a way to get to know Nestlé better and expand my financial and leadership skills. Since I had worked with some of my colleagues at Nestlé on various projects, they spoke up for me. They vouched for my broad financial skills, but also noted my communication and interpersonal skills – traits that would be necessary to working in the headquarters of an international company and in a market outside my own. I didn't have to prove myself to get the job: I was a known quantity, which made both getting the job and making the transition so much easier.

Anna

After approximately ten years of excellent experience at Amoco in sales and marketing – a textbook career path, but one similar to that taken by most of my peers – I knew I had to differentiate myself somehow. With supervisors and senior management who would listen, I began to seed my conversations with my desire to use my Mandarin language skills in business, specifically to be part of any expansion in China. Although I had performed extremely well, I did not assume that I would get considered for the same opportunities as men. People recommend and advocate for individuals in large part because they can "picture" them in the job. Those making decisions have a hard time picturing people who are different from themselves in these positions. As most leaders are men, women don't generally receive equal consideration without a conscious intervention process. So I worked it, making sure that I communicated far and wide within the organization my desire, my credibility, and my skills. Within a few years, my efforts paid off. When Amoco considered opening a downstream office in China, my name came up. But because I was pregnant with my second child and had a husband who worked, some in management didn't think I was right for the job. Luckily for me, I had an advocate in the room, someone who knew that I had expressed strong interest in working in China. This person recommended that rather than assume I wouldn't go, they should ask me – just in case. When I learned of this opportunity, I made it clear to my boss that I would like to be considered and that as long as my child was born healthy I would go.

I knew I could excel in the role for several reasons. One, I had the language skills and cultural understanding, which would be helpful in picking up innuendos and dealing with local employees in China. Second, I had certain traits that I believed would be critical to working successfully overseas, specifically my ability to adapt and build teams, as well as my management style characterized by collaboration, enthusiasm, and an optimistic attitude – skills not always valued in a traditional "command-and-control" environment in which new managers come in to take over and keep things running "as is." Most importantly, I knew that I was supported by a wonderful husband and family, willing to take the risk and looking forward to an adventure!

Patricia

I had done my research and knew that western news organizations in Russia needed more reporters on the ground in the early 1990s. The Soviet Union was opening up, history was being made, and there was a hunger in the West to learn more about what was going on behind the once-impenetrable Iron Curtain. But the Soviet government refused to increase the small number of visas allotted to British and American journalists, who up to then had been forced to live in guarded compounds that were off limits to average Russians. That meant that news outlets either missed stories or tried to find local hires who could speak the language. I felt I had a good shot at getting hired by a big-name western media company because I spoke Russian, I was inexpensive as a local hire, and I could get the job done well.

I landed in Moscow in the summer of 1990, and the first thing I did was set about finding a place to stay. At that time – and even more so today – Moscow was very expensive for expats. However, I knew I could manage the financials of supporting myself if I lived like a Russian. My Russian teacher's friends allowed me to stay in their apartment in the center of Moscow for the summer while the owner lived in her dacha (summer country house). The location was excellent and the price cheap. I had managed to rent out my apartment in Washington, D.C., for more than my mortgage, and so I felt good about my financial progress. Within a week of arriving, I was settled, meeting people and finding my way around. I started making the rounds at all the foreign news outlets, letting them know of my credentials, my language skills, and my instant availability. In a few short weeks, I was hired as a stringer for *U.S. News & World Report* and later Reuters for the same. My dream of being a foreign correspondent had finally come true.

By the end of the summer, I had to find another apartment, as well as convince *U.S. News & World Report* to sponsor my business visa, which came with multiple entries and press accreditation – which it did. I was paid well and in U.S. dollars, critical to a non-Russian's financial well-being at the time. It was important to me that I live within my means while on the ground, which I did and quite comfortably. I stayed for 15 months before I decided to return to the United States – but just for a while.

Chapter 4

Ready, Set, Go!

When making a move abroad, never underestimate the amount of administrative details you must deal with – many times in a hurry. You'll be dealing with two countries and the various customs, laws, taxation, and so on. Satisfying all the requirements sometimes feels like a full-time job all by itself. So be sure to take the time to negotiate the right assignment and best package. Doing so will help a great deal in setting you up for success.

– Jackie, Alcon

Once you accept an international posting or agree to move and start a new life in another land, your daily routine will be overtaken by a whirlwind of activity. Typically, you will be required to continue to fulfill your existing professional duties while learning about what's awaiting you at your next destination. In addition, you'll be managing the personal aspects of moving, such as selling your home or subletting your apartment, taking care of the various financial and legal elements involved in moving overseas, and pursuing the more mundane but demanding task of packing up. Do not lose heart, no matter how stressed you might feel through this transition phase.

Practically speaking, you need to stay organized to stay on track. The way to put your best international foot forward is to properly plan and prepare before you accept the position. From evaluating the assignment to negotiating a fair contract to packing up and moving, there are some best practices to follow, so read on to pick up tips from the experts.

Ready? Evaluate the Assignment

In this chapter, we'll evaluate the two basic kinds of international relocations. The first is one in which a company transfers you to another country. The second is moving yourself to another country without having already secured a job or position. Both need careful, objective consideration and demand a thoughtful approach to learning all you can about where you are going. To help you differentiate, though, we'll discuss each in turn.

Nonprofit or Government Transfers

Most of the advice given throughout this book applies to corporate international assignments. While there are many similarities in the experiences, one difference lies in the transfer. Government positions usually have standard packages with little or no room for negotiation. Nonprofit organizations may offer a simple, no-frills package. Use the information in this chapter as a guide, but do not be surprised if what is standard for the private sector is not the same as what is covered by government or a nonprofit organization. For more information, go to your own government-sponsored Web sites or the global nonprofit organizations' Web sites.

If you are fortunate enough to be offered an opportunity to be transferred overseas, be sure you get an accurate picture of the position and your responsibilities before you accept. Your first step is to clarify the following ten points in as much detail as practical, keeping in mind that this list covers the most important elements when you are considering the offer. Some are appropriate for contracts and some are not. To that end, we recommend a list of line items that constitute a thorough package further on in the chapter.

Top Ten Tips
for the Aspiring International Executive

1. **Your position.** Request a detailed job description, including the exact title, roles, responsibilities, and the key objectives by which your performance will be measured. If you have a team, be apprised of their

levels and titles, years of experience, reporting lines if not 100 percent to you, and overall roles in the office or plant and on your team. You can use this document in your annual performance review. It will also come in very handy if management changes during your time abroad.

2. **Length of your assignment.** There should be a minimum and maximum time allocation for your assignment and a clear delineation of what happens if either is not met. It is in everybody's best interest to have a plan in place should the opportunity to extend the assignment arise. To that end, determine what criteria would be used to make that extension, and leave yourself some flexibility in case you decide to stay on.

3. **Your reporting structure.** Find out specifically to whom you report and where that person is based. Although it is not part of the contract, you'll also want to know your supervisor's experience, background, and nationality and – important to try to determine – whether you can learn from this person.

4. **Your expected work schedule.** The number of hours in a typical work day differs in markets around the world, as do the number of days in a work week and the days that constitute a weekend (e.g., some weekends are Saturday and Sunday; some are Friday and Saturday). Many times, whether it is formally stated or not, you will be expected to work both the local schedule as well as that of the parent company. In addition, be sure to clarify how much travel, either in-country or out of it, is expected of you.

5. **Your new office culture and climate.** Ask as many questions as you can about the internal culture and environment of the office or plant in which you'll be based, including what issues, problems, successes and/or failures this location has had in the last eighteen months. You'll be better positioned to understand how you might be able to make a difference. For instance, if you're expected to be the heroine of a horror story, you'll be gearing up differently than if you're expected to be one of several expats being transferred into an already successful location.

6. **Cross-cultural training.** Confirm whether you will have the opportunity to undergo cross-cultural training before your departure. Alt-

hough some companies have a solid indoctrination program as part of the expat package, many don't. If yours doesn't, consider requesting it as part of your package, as studies show that employees who receive solid cross-cultural training tend to transition much better both into a new market and back to the old. There are companies that specialize in cross-cultural training.

Making It Real

I was sent to Beijing to open Amoco's first representative office. As such, the company provided some great expatriate induction programs that covered logistics and moving, which were critical to my eventual success. Yet, when I was transferred to London years later, my indoctrination paled in comparison. I guess people didn't think the British culture needed much explaining and probably didn't think much of it, as it was the HQ. But I would caution anyone considering a move to London to seek out people who have lived there before, and do not assume the culture and language are the same as they are in America – they aren't.

– Anna, former BP executive

7. **Site visit.** Determine whether you will be allowed at least one company-sponsored site visit before you accept the offer – preferably with your spouse or significant other if you have one – to explore your potential new home. You'll need to spend at least three days, although a full week is even better. If the company doesn't allow such a visit, you should request the opportunity to talk to a few people who've lived there, preferably on assignment with the company, so you can gather their valuable information. Or consider financing your own visit if you can afford it. In addition, search Web sites, rent tapes, and read guide books both before and after your site visit (or in place of it, if necessary).

8. **Long-term plan.** Clarify what the company expects of you when you return, including an indication that you will have a position that is either equal to your role in the new market or a promotion. In addition, request that you be considered for a position that capitalizes on your international skills. Sometimes you may need to stay a bit longer or leave a little early to get the next plum assignment, but if both you

and your company want to make the most of your international business experience, it will probably come to pass.

9. **Reasons for the transfer.** Do your best to determine all the reasons the company is transferring you and why it believes you'll be successful. Ask questions of HR, your current supervisor, and others who have been involved in the decision-making process, including the local team in the country and region in which you'll be working. You'll want to find out what they expect of you, and the best way to find out is to ask – preferably before or during the site visit. Many times you'll find that what your head office expects of you is different from what the local office wants or needs. A certain amount of this dynamic tension is to be expected. However, you want to be sure the two positions are not completely at odds with each other, as this will put you in the middle of a lose-lose situation. In addition, ask why your company – both HQ and the local hiring team – believes that you will be successful. Understanding their expectations before you agree can prove critical to success.

10. **Effect on Spouse and Children.** If you are married and/or have children, you must determine whether this position will enable you to adequately fulfill your personal responsibilities. Many times, overseas postings include a great deal of travel, long days, and lots of evening entertaining. Only you can decide if you'll be able to manage, though many women have done so – and extremely well. Throughout the book, we share advice and anecdotes of this important component to arm you with as much information as possible to make this personal decision.

Companies change, and the people with whom you are negotiating today may not be in the same position – or even the same company – tomorrow. Therefore, it is critical to get as much in writing as possible. After clarifying the answers to the ten points previously listed and considering the relevant pros and cons, re-ask yourself the list of questions in Chapter 2. Is there anything about the nature of the assignment that raises red flags? Do you anticipate any major problems? If so, talk with your HR representative about your concerns, and determine if there is some course of action to be taken so that, together, you can sort through if the issue you've identified will be fatal to your success overseas. Remember, it is in no one's interest for you to fail. It's best to go into the situation with your eyes wide open. Once you've secured answers to the questions above, request that the relevant specifics be included in your contract.

Ready? Evaluate the Location

In Chapter 3, you learned how to target markets. You can use this list again to evaluate the country to which you are being transferred – and even use it to pick one country or city over another if you are being given a choice.

Ten Things to Consider When Picking a Market

1. Business needs
2. Personal interest
3. Personal comfort (safety, culture, environment, and health)
4. Cost of living
5. Language skills
6. Up-and-coming hot spots (i.e., business opportunity)
7. Familiarity
8. Heritage
9. Region vs. one country
10. Family factor

Look Before You Leap!

If you are granted the opportunity to visit the place before you move, do it. This investment will pay off for both you and your employer because you will either reconfirm your ability to successfully move and work there or you will learn something about the place that would make it difficult for you to do so. Such a visit can include business orientation activities, such as meeting the local team, touring plants or facilities, meeting clients or customers, and social engagements with local or regional HR, leadership, and future supervisors. If there are other expats in the office, try to meet with them as well, both formally and informally.

This trip can serve many other purposes, as well, including satisfying your personal curiosity about various elements of your new life. You can go on an apartment-hunting or house-hunting tour with realtors or check out a corporate apartment owned by your employer. You can visit schools, shopping malls, and grocery stores to get an idea of what you might need to bring or buy. You can go on day tours and get a feel for the place. You can wander the streets and take public transportation to begin to get your bearings. If you coordinate and plan your activities before you leave, you won't waste your first few weeks on the ground with mundane practicalities.

Making It Real

Before I moved, I visited Hong Kong three times for a combination of client-related business and pre-move trip. Business and personal matters were taken care of: I met my future team and made time to get a feel for the place. I went hunting for a flat and took pictures of various buildings, views, and floor plans; toured and wandered the streets day and night, snapping pictures everywhere. The sense of the place came through so that by the time the moving truck arrived, I was sure I could live there. Sharing the photos of the flats with my husband, who wasn't able to join me on the trips turned out well. Our little paradise was known as the Chinese Riviera; our thirteenth-floor view overlooked Dragon's Back Mountain, which rose up dramatically from the crystal blue sea below.

– Stacie, coauthor and consultant

Use your site visit wisely, and make sure you check out the following:

- **Housing.** Before you go, ask HR about your housing allowance and/or guidelines in which to search for a place to live. Try to make contact with a realtor before you arrive. If you are moving to a city that has ultra-high rents like Tokyo, Hong Kong, Moscow, or London, you will probably be "equalized" or asked to pay the same in rent that you paid in your home country be it a monthly rent or mortgage. If you are not given an allowance and must pay on your own, determine your budget and ask the realtor for his most creative options. Make sure you know where your work location is, orient yourself with a map, and seek advice on commute times and other options. Ask colleagues about the best places to live, given your personal circumstances, or visit your local consulate or embassy for information.

- **Household items.** Take a short detour through a department store and local grocery store. Cruise the aisles looking for your favorite products. Make a note of those you can't find, as well as the type of appliances and the voltage; there are two types: 110V and 220V. Electrical outlets differ in many places, and although a universal adaptor for your computer and mobile phone are essential for travel, major appliances – even hair dryers – often won't work effectively through them for long. Therefore, it's usually more practical to buy the necessary appliances locally rather than transport them.

- **Schools and daycare.** If you have children, take the time to visit the local schools or daycare they could attend. All major cities have daycare and international schools. Some even offer major national schools, such as the Japanese School in Greenwich, Connecticut (for postings in or around New York City), the French school of Detroit, Michigan, and the German Swiss International School Hong Kong. Make sure that you meet not only the administrators, such as the headmaster or principal, but also some of the teachers and caregivers in your child's age group. Also ask for referrals of parents with children of similar age and background, and try to connect, at least by phone if not in person. Note the location and your transportation needs, including drop-off and pick-up times. Are there after-school programs, such as sports, music, or creative arts? Learning about options and planning ahead the logistics of your child's days will be important to everyone's successful initial adjustment. Also, find out what, if any, medical forms and vaccinations you will need to have completed before your children can start the program. Of course, the cost may be higher than back home, so be sure to find out the total cost per child – not just tuition but meals, books, special activities, and the like – and consider this financial aspect as part of your decision-making process.

Making It Real

In addition to checking out schools and speaking directly with another parent, find out if there are opportunities for your children to continue to learn their native language.

– Annica, Kraft Foods, Inc.

- **Health Care.** Access to good medical care is important and should not be sacrificed. Your employer should have information on the topic, but the best way to determine if the local care is acceptable is to ask people in similar situations. Fellow expats are a good source, as are any contacts you may have at your consulate or embassy. Although many people find health care options in the developing world not on par with those in the developed world, most expatriates are able to find reasonable care for all routine matters. If possible, visit a hospital or establish contact with a well-regarded physician during your site visit. Check out the necessary immunizations for all family members, not only in your new home country but also in any countries within the region to which you might be traveling.

- **The daily life basics.** Find out as much as you can about the various aspects of daily life, including the following:
  - ✓ **Local currency.** What is it? Is the rate fixed, pegged to the U.S. dollar, or variable? Request to be paid only in a stable currency or in U.S. dollars, but be cognizant of the fact that the dollar fluctuates, too, especially in comparison to the Euro and the British pound.
  - ✓ **Banking institutions.** What are the better-known banks? Choose one that maintains branches within the region, at least, and possibly in your home country as well.
  - ✓ **Taxation.** What are the various taxes you could owe, such as income or property? Are there municipal, provincial, and national taxes? Is there one flat tax, or does the rate vary? Is there a tax treaty with your country to obviate your paying any tax? Will you be tax equalized by your company?
  - ✓ **Health insurance.** Are there government-sponsored health plans, or is all coverage private? Do most companies sponsor

employees, or is it typical to participate on your own? What is the coverage like, and how does it differ from what you are used to?

✓ **Transportation.** Is public transportation, such as buses, underground, or trolleys, safe and easy to use? If not, request that your employer cover a private car or taxi service. With respect to taxis, find out if there is a general corporate policy about using local taxis and which companies are preferred.

✓ **Food and Water.** Is tap water safe to drink? Are there any guidelines to follow re: eating in restaurants? From street vendors?

✓ **Shopping.** What are the shops like? Are there supermarkets, large chain retail outlets, or small local markets? Are there shopping malls or places where people buy certain goods? Do the prices seem comparable to those back home? (Tip: take a pocket calculator if need be when you're just getting accustomed to using the currency.)

✓ **Laws.** Are there any laws that stand out as unusual? For example, in Singapore, it's against the law to chew gum and or to not flush public toilets.

Making It Real

Gather as much information as you can from a variety of sources – the Web, newspapers, books, and articles recommended by HR and friends. If possible, talk to folks who have already worked in the region you're going to. The U.S. Chamber of Commerce, which maintains a well-established network overseas, has terrific information for all foreign locations. Don't forget about the embassy in the country you're considering. Once you're posted, they offer citizens a host of services from security, safety, and medical updates to professional contacts.

– **Mary, FAA**

• **Safety.** What is the crime rate? Are the streets safe? Are there hate crimes or specific tensions among ethnic or religious groups? Are you any more likely to be a target because you are a woman, specifically a foreign woman? What do other women do to stay safe?

- **Religion.** Is there a predominant religion? Is the country tolerant of your religion? Will you be able to practice your religion and feel comfortable doing so? Is there a house of worship that suits your needs?

Working Spouses

If your spouse is moving with you, it's important that you establish whether he can work and/or under what circumstances and restrictions. Each country is different. Employers sometimes offer to help a spouse find work, secure a work visa, or put him in touch with other multinationals. If your spouse can't work or isn't permitted to, this new-found freedom may be just what he wanted – or may be the worst years of his life. Make sure that both of you know his options before you accept the offer. If possible, include career assistance for your spouse in your contract.

Making It Real

We knew right from the get-go that Ed wouldn't be able to work in either Switzerland or Belgium. He was OK with that, and after living with him for almost five years while he occupied himself with a combination of intellectual pursuits, various sports, and traveling, I'm pretty sure I'll know what he'll be like when he retires – not a bad thing to learn about your husband early on!

– **Diane, DuPont**

Set? Consider Contracts and Compensation

The glory days of plum expat assignments are fading or available only to the most senior executives or to those who move to uncharted markets, such as the Middle East or Africa. Rightfully, most companies view international assignments as a means by which you can grow and advance your career, so more and more professionals are required to move abroad for a few years without the myriad perks that used to accompany these moves. Huge financial packages are often no longer necessary to lure the best candidates. That's why it's more important than ever that you understand the financial components of your transfer and negotiate the best deal. Included below are the key elements to an expatriate contract. When you receive your contract, carefully review it. We've included a list of line items constituting a thorough package that would probably be offered in a hardship posting or to a more senior executive. If yours doesn't include all of these but some are important to you, it never hurts to ask. Remember, the agreement must be considered fair and equitable by both sides. If you feel the slightest doubt about what you're signing, be sure to have a qualified attorney and/or financial advisor or accountant review the contract and explain clearly any items you don't completely understand. Key components include the following:

- **Start date**
- **Length of assignment**, including repercussions if you leave early or leave the company
- **Compensation**
  - ✓ **Base salary**, which may include a slight bump to recognize a promotion but probably not reflect the additional monies needed to live in your new country
  - ✓ **Bonus**, which may be structured differently from your current one; make sure it is at least equal to what you have now
  - ✓ **COLA** (cost of living adjustment), which rounds up your compensation to reflect the additional monies necessary to live abroad if there are any (may exclude rent)
  - ✓ **Retirement benefits**, such as pension, 401(k), and others, which should remain at least equal to what you already receive
  - ✓ **Insurance**, such as various types of health care, dental, and life, should reflect equal coverage and not less
  - ✓ **Stock options and grants**, which should continue to be offered at the same level that you've received previously
  - ✓ **Payment**, which could be local currency or home country's currency (Tip: If offered a choice, go with the most stable currency)
  - ✓ **Vacations/holidays**, which should remain the same number or be increased if the standard policy in your new country allows for more; you should not get fewer than you've earned to date, and ideally, you should get more as you'll need time to visit those friends and family you left behind
  - ✓ **Tax equalization** depends on your nationality, but you should not pay more taxes in your new home than you would in your

old, especially with the increased compensation due to market differences

- **Allowances** are not included as part of your regular compensation so that when you return, you do not feel as though your salary has diminished

  ✓ **Combat pay** (also referred to as hardship pay), which is a sum over and above your base salary and given because you are going to an extremely difficult location and/or are being asked to do an extraordinary assignment

  ✓ **Relocation allowance**, which covers the purchase of local appliances and household items that aren't worth shipping but that you still need

  ✓ **Housing allowance/equalization**, which many companies will provide if the rent differences are great or if buying a house is more prudent

  ✓ **Property sale/management**, if you plan to sell or rent your existing home and/or plan to buy a home in your new country

  ✓ **Car**, which can be either your own company car or a car and driver, if necessary, in markets where safety is an issue (such as Bogota) or the driving extremely difficult because of traffic congestion (such as Bangkok)

  ✓ **Schooling or daycare** for children, which many companies will cover if the cost of the equivalent local programs is greater than your costs back home.

Making It Real

If BP hadn't agreed to pay for schooling for my two children while in London, it would have been a deal-breaker for me. I believe that schooling is one of the most important benefits a company can pay for – second only to access to good medical care.

– Anna, former BP executive

  ✓ **Home leave**, which most companies offer once a year, depending on your seniority and family circumstances

  ✓ **Medivac/emergency travel insurance**, which is important for all employees, especially those traveling to "trouble spots"

✓ **Emergency leave**, which provides a clause that if you must return home for an emergency, the company will pay for you and your family to travel, in addition to your home leave

✓ **Tax Planning**, which allows for a qualified accountant either on retainer to your company or chosen by you to prepare your taxes locally and, if necessary, back in your home country. When you are dealing with the tax codes of possibly two countries, having a professional assist you is an important service. For instance, the majority of the items noted above are considered "income" to be added to your individual compensation, but they are calculated differently than straight dollars earned. The complexity can be quite daunting and time consuming.

Making It Real

Taxes in a foreign jurisdiction can be complicated – be sure to have access to an experienced professional. As an American – even as an experienced financial professional – I found that filing my U.S. tax return as an expat was not a piece of cake. I found it easier to do my own Swiss return, in French, than to do my United States return.

— **Jackie, Alcon**

- **Cross-cultural training**, which provides for in-depth training of you and your family, if possible, on the ins and outs of the new culture. In addition, this training should be included upon your return home as well – an often overlooked but small price to pay for helping employees repatriate properly.

- **Relocation**
  ✓ **Real estate assistance,** depending on your personal needs. If you currently own your home, you may decide to sell it or rent it while you're gone, and if you plan to either buy or rent a home in your new country, you'll need professional assistance to identify and recommend a reputable company or pay any fees related to real estate expenses.
  ✓ **Moving expenses**, which covers the packing and shipping of your personal goods by container and usually includes some air

shipments for the essentials you'll need immediately upon arrival. Those goods you do not want shipped will be stored and insured as well.

- ✓ **Temporary living expenses**, which provides a place for you and your family to stay upon arrival, even if you have rented a home or apartment. It usually takes a week to get settled in, and if your goods have been shipped, they won't arrive for several weeks: four to twelve weeks is standard, depending on your location.
- ✓ **On-site assistance**, which will help orient you in your new location. Sometimes company HR departments can handle your orientation.

- **Repatriation**
  - ✓ **Job security** means that you will have a position upon your return. Do your best to get further guarantees of a position and base salary at the same level as, or higher than, than your posting.
  - ✓ **Services**, such temporary housing, rental cars, cross-cultural training, and air shipments of specific special effects, should be detailed according to your personal needs.

A significant change we've noticed in companies' international relocation policies is an increase in terms limits. Many companies are limiting expat status to three years and either repatriating the employee, moving her to another location, or offering a local hire package. Becoming a local hire has its pros and cons, and many times it's the only way to remain in a country. If you choose to go this route, you will forfeit such things as home leave, housing expenses, tax equalization, and sometimes even retirement and pension programs based in your own country. It's important that you understand the short-term and long-term financial aspects of becoming a local hire. Many times if you "go local," regardless of how well you negotiate, you may be less financially well off in the short term, but you may end up at a financial advantage in the future because of the greater possibilities that open up. You must be able to weigh the short term against the long term. Companies recognize the challenges and many are changing their policies. For instance, "The WPP group of companies operates as a truly global organization, and our international relocations are no exception," said Stephen McGarry, director of global mobility at WPP. "We have adapted both our policies and our terminology to reflect our global citizenry, for example, no longer transferring 'expats' but sending people on global assignment. Our companies' compensation packages no longer reflect a UK- or U.S.-based scheme only; we have regional policies and packages that better address the needs of our global workforce. These seemingly small changes have made a big difference in the success of our program."

Making It Real

If you plan on becoming a local hire, do your research. Although the rewards can be great, it could cost you a lot of money, unnecessarily, if you don't get the financials right.

— **Jackie, Alcon**

Moving Without an Assignment

Some of you may feel a strong desire to move on your own, without a company assignment. Perhaps you have recently finished college or want to hone your language skills by living abroad, or perhaps you have just returned from a vacation in a place that you feel you must revisit. Whatever the reason, if you feel passionately about it, prepare and plan properly, and are willing to take some risks, you can do it. It will become self-evident which points in this chapter apply to your situation. Use it before you go, as well as once you're on the ground negotiating your employment contract. You might also find it helpful if you are hired locally but are transferred by your new employer to another country or back home. Each situation is different, so use your best judgment. You'll be operating on your own, at least for a while. Here are a few tips: be sure to cover them in your premove planning and preparation and as you take your first steps upon arriving.

Ready, Set?
- Understand the local laws regarding work visas and taxation.
- Have a strong command of the local language.
- Have a resourceful and responsible go-to person on the ground.

- Research cost-of-living expenses, and confirm your ability to meet them for at least three months without pay.
- Research medical insurance, local health care options, and, if necessary, Medivac or evacuation insurance.
- Create a contact list, asking as many people as possible who they may know on the ground.

Go!

- Make contact with your consulate or embassy upon arriving.
- Choose a safe place to live.
- Pack only what you can carry.
- Do not bring unnecessary valuables in case it takes you a while to find a place to live.
- Network like crazy!

Making It Real

If you move overseas to look for a job locally, your odds of finding one increase significantly. Your move alone will prove to prospective employers that (1) you are committed to being there, (2) you have initiative, and (3) you are adventurous and have a certain tolerance for risk.

– Penny, ABN AMRO

Go! Packing and Preparing Checklists

Sorting and Packing

- Scale back and clean house – less is more.
  - ✓ Bring only essentials – and that is less than you think.
  - ✓ Put in storage only what you believe you need for your return (i.e., don't be a pack rat).
  - ✓ Give nonessentials away or donate to local charities.
- Select a few items to give your new place a touch of home, such as photos, special pictures.
- If you have children, be sure to bring some things to keep them in touch with their roots, such as native language books, videos, holiday decorations, and traditional nonperishable foods.

- Pack essential personal care items, such as eye care products, prescriptions, and even special make-up needs, enough for at least six months (twelve is better).
- Bring small, inexpensive gifts – the little things *are* important – from your home country to give out on occasion, such as American baseball hats or coffee mugs, matrushka dolls from Russia, and origami from Japan.

Making It Real

You're going to buy things, and you'll need a place to put them. Pack less and store more, and make sure you've got the right-size container for your return. Most of us returned with two to three times the amount we brought.

– Perry, coauthor and Kraft Foods, Inc.

I took a few things that reminded me of my roots, such as an old stuffed animal and a baby blanket that my great-aunt made for me. You'd be surprised how, when the adventure stops being all about your future, you start realizing that you are letting go of pieces of your past. We girls need a couple of real, comfortable reminders around us of who we really are.

– Pamela, The Teagarden Group

I moved from an apartment in New York that was four hundred square feet to one in Singapore that was twenty-four hundred square feet – and I filled it with amazing Asian antiques. My antique wedding bed from Shanghai is bigger than my old NY studio apartment!

– Joanne, USAID

We brought our two cats to Switzerland and returned five years later with a Bernese mountain dog. He was 135 pounds when we brought him back to the United States from Belgium, and he had a huge crate built for him to travel in.

– Diane, DuPont

Legal Paperwork

- Update your will and power of attorney.
- Convey your emergency contact information to your employer.
- Insure valuables.

94

- Contact your brokerage house regarding your move and ongoing investments.
- Forward your mail and cancel subscriptions that won't be forwarded abroad.

Medical Check-up

- Get an annual checkup before you leave (all family members).
- Get all required inoculations for your country (all family members) and for those you might be traveling to in the next six months (consider the same for all family members).
- Fill prescriptions for at least twelve months, if the medicine is shelf stable.
- Bring copies of essential medical records (all family members).

Making It Real

Besides grabbing the practical essentials, like medical and dental records, I also asked my hairdresser to show me how he did things for me – I assumed Siberia would not have a ton of salons. He taught me how to dye my own hair, and showed me some easy styles I could do for myself. It was pretty funny to watch the faces of the people in my Houston salon while I was doing my own hair with him watching. And then I paid him! He even took me to the grocery store to decide the home color I should buy in bulk to bring with me. I figured, Siberia is *not* the place for bad hair days!

– Pamela, The Teagarden Group

Important Documents to Carry with You

- Passports, visas and/or work permits
- Birth certificates
- Marriage, divorce, child custody, and adoption papers
- Driver's license
- Medical and dental records
- Shipping/packing documents and insurance
- Eye glass prescription and a spare pair

The Journey Continues

Anna

I was six months pregnant when I agreed to move to China, and so it wasn't practical to do a site visit. Most physicians and insurance companies don't let pregnant women travel by air after seven and a half months. International travel is even more difficult, and long stretches of time on a plane can be extremely uncomfortable. When we landed as a family for our two-year stint, my son was three months old. We lived in a hotel for six months because it took that long to set up Amoco's representative office, which was a prerequisite to signing rental papers and importing personal goods. Although we entertained the idea of renting our house back in the United States, we decided to sell, not wanting the hassle of being overseas landlords. The company had a buy-out program that worked out well. We were pretty sure we wouldn't return to the same house – probably not even the same city – so we sold the house and put our furniture in storage.

My experience in China taught me very quickly not to sweat the small stuff. I had to set up an office – something I had never done before and certainly not in a foreign city. I was shocked by the reality of how difficult maneuvering through the complicated process was. Not only was it tricky to comprehend the steps to securing real estate and purchasing (in our case building) furnishings, but there were also so many procedures regarding recruiting and hiring nationals that needed to be understood. I quickly learned that the three most important aspects of setting up an office are location, technology, and local know-how. First, location matters, especially if you want to make a good impression with partners, clients, and potential employees – as well as access to Western amenities in a city like Beijing. Second, technology can be so different in various parts of the world, sometimes frustratingly inadequate or slow, so I believed it critical to build out our technology capabilities. It made a huge difference in our connectivity to HQ and the rest of the world. Third, whether it's to help you set up and run your office or your household, get a strong "go-to" national who can help you maneuver through the hoops and figure out the system. I could have wasted a lot of time spinning my wheels – especially in China, where relationships matter a great deal – if my staff hadn't helped me figure out how to get things done. Once the business was up and running, I was comfortably able to leverage my ability to speak Mandarin into a real strategic advantage.

After such a positive experience in China, I felt as though London would be easy. Contrary to our expectations, London was not a cakewalk. The adjustment of living in Central London – including driving, parking, shopping, finding workmen – turned out to be more of a challenge than we anticipated. One should not expect the conveniences of America just because you're in a country that is considered first world and speaks relatively the same language. Nevertheless, we enjoyed our time there. We rented for the first two years and then ended up buying a flat, which we renovated during the last three years. Although many expats don't buy, it can pay off handsomely if you do find yourself in an appreciating real estate market with a favorable exchange rate. With the renovation project, we were also able to incorporate many "U.S. amenities" into our flat, such as a full-sized laundry room and an oversized kitchen, both of which are nearly impossible to find in Europe.

Diane

I accepted the offer and within three months was working and living in

Geneva. Prior to our move, I spent a few weeks there working with colleagues getting into the Swiss groove. I had been on the ground about five days when my husband, Ed, joined me for a whirlwind, two-day tour of real estate. Upon landing, Ed (who does not do well on overnight flights) desperately needed a coffee. Our realtor, an efficient and prompt Swiss woman, insisted we did not have time to stop for a coffee. Ed just wanted an American-sized coffee-to-go, which he quickly learned did not exist in Geneva. We stopped and sat down for a coffee and when the waitress brought out a small espresso-size cup, I signaled to her and asked for another six! I could tell that Ed was wondering what kind of place didn't have coffee to go in super-sizes, but if that gave him pause, he didn't say anything. He didn't have time – our realtor was pushing us out the door to view more than twenty properties that day. Being on time really matters in Switzerland! After those two days, we finally found a house we liked.

Our next step was to rent our house. When it came to deciding whether to sell or rent, we didn't think twice. Ed had just built our house, and we had only lived in it for six months. It's difficult being an overseas landlord, and Ed went home once, sometimes twice, a year to inspect it even though we had property management assistance. We had both a good and bad experience with renting. We had one resident renter for the entire five years we were gone; that's the positive – sort of. Not enough due diligence was done on him and his background, however, and at the end of the lease, he owed back rent for many months because of a host of personal and financial problems. We personally lost about $10,000 on the whole deal and that accounts for the amount DuPont contributed to ease our pain. But sometimes selling is not an option. The house holds a special place in our hearts; we still live in it today and love it! We recommend you seek professional advice about the real estate market and make a financial decision about whether to sell or rent based on the macroeconomic picture and personal needs. Sometimes people sell their houses on the cusp of a boom, and when they return, they can't afford their old house, let alone the new ones for sale. With the minimal amount we shipped with us, we were able to bring back probably twice as many goods in the container home – treasures that reflect our international lifestyle – and bring back many warm memories of our years in Europe.

Jackie

Before I moved to Switzerland, I made several trips there. Each trip was between one and three weeks long and proved to be a big help in ensuring a smooth move. I took care of both professional and personal moving-related matters: I got to know the area by getting out and walking a lot, taking public transportation, and spending time with friends and colleagues who lived in the region and showed me around. I got a car, set up a bank account, got insurance, and learned where to shop. I found a place to live so I could move right in. I took measurements of the rooms, as well as photos to be sure anything I shipped would fit. There's a difference between Texas-size and European size! I also learned about my new role, working my way into it so I better understood what was expected of me. When I actually started my new position, most of my personal arrangements were in place, which made starting my new job so much easier.

I lived in Switzerland for nine years – three as an Alcon expat, five as a local Nestlé employee, and one as a local Swissair employee. Each had its advantages. I went local with Nestlé because I was offered a great position but as a local hire. Although I probably didn't learn all that I could have about the differences, I took the plunge, confident it would benefit my overall career. It did, and as I look back, I consider myself lucky that nothing went awry and I didn't suffer any financial setbacks. The potential ramifications of changing employers can be complicated. I trusted Nestlé, and things worked out ok. I gave up the perks of home leave, tax equalization, and housing, which I found to be minor changes in comparison to the retirement and pension programs and the self-sufficiency that was expected of me. All of a sudden, the services I had grown comfortable with were no longer part of the deal. But I managed just fine, learning how to do both my U.S. expatriate tax return and my Swiss return in French. I paid Swiss Social Security and contributed to the Swiss-based company pension fund that, after the required vesting period, I was able to transfer from Nestlé to Swissair when I changed local Swiss employers. Switching employers as a noncitizen presented a different set of challenges altogether because I didn't have the same support network around me as I did as a transferred employee. I had to deal with my own administrative requirements of changing location within country – and in a new language, German.

When I eventually left several years ago, I chose to leave my retirement contributions in place until I reached Switzerland's retirement age. If I choose, I can liquidate before that time, but at significant tax consequences in both Switzerland and the United States. Financially, it's probably best to keep it there but this means I must relinquish a certain amount of control: I have no say in how a sizeable portion of my retirement is invested, it's exposed to currency fluctuations, and I have to keep track of it separately as opposed to a consolidated financial plan. This level of complexity makes it a bit more challenging to be a local hire, but for me, the benefits have far exceeded the risks. As a financial person, I'm comfortable with foreign currency markets and can manage multiple accounts. I do get a little nervous, however, when I think of having to return to Switzerland in my 60s and complete all the paperwork necessary to get my retirement monies out. Keeping up the languages is important!

Stacie

I was so excited about the potential move that although I reviewed my assignment letter, which included most of the items listed in this chapter, I didn't bother to do much research into whether what I was signing was outstanding, fair, or below par. I didn't even think to negotiate any additional components that, I found out later, many friends and colleagues did. I trusted B-M, and I was lucky: everything turned out very well. Interestingly, I received a significant raise when I moved because (a) my U.S. salary was below par for my level in Asia-Pacific, and (b) I was being asked to take on a greater leadership role. My first international eye-opener came as I discussed salaries over a fine Chinese dinner in Hong Kong with the regional HR director during my site visit. He said that I was underpaid and that B-M Asia was going to right things. I was struck with the disparity between how much more money I would be paid to work for the same company in a different country: combination of base salary plus bonus was 50 to 60 percent higher than in Washington, D.C.

I felt really good about the assignment, but then reality hit. In just three short months I would need to wrap up and transition my current assignments; sort, pack, move, and store personal goods with a relatively new partner of three years; remotely plan a wedding to take place in Miami the weekend before we moved; and continue to make two more Hong Kong-Washington, D.C., trips for a client. Those eighteen-hour flights to Hong Kong proved to be the best planning time periods I could have asked for! I used every minute to make thorough, thoughtful, yet fast decisions, and read up on Hong Kong. I even shopped for and bought my wedding dress one afternoon in Hong Kong.

When it came to packing, I think we probably put too much in storage and should have "cleaned house" a little better. But we did make the right decision when it came to shipping; Mike and I didn't ship much furniture, agreeing instead to rent a sparsely furnished flat and acquire local items. I'm so glad we did, because after three years and numerous purchases from the antique stores, we have an eclectic mix of Chinese and nineteenth-century American furniture, art, and china.

Perry

After three years in Singapore, I agreed to trade sun for snow and moved to Moscow. Having moved to Singapore, I already had no home, no car, no pets, and no permanent boyfriend, so those were not an issue. It would be hard to imagine a more difficult move, but in some ways, it made the packing a lot easier; there was virtually nothing to take from Singapore to Moscow. But there were a lot of things I needed to buy – coats, hats, snow shoes, long johns. I hadn't had to worry about cold for years, but I was going to a place renowned for its long, bone-chilling winters. I decided that since Russia was a relatively difficult logistics market, it was best not to try to bring a whole houseful of goods. With that said, I did note during my pre-move visit the things I would not be able to find when I landed, and I packed accordingly. I focused on bringing the things that provided a real sense of comfort and security – like my favorite down blanket, pillows, and flannel sheets.

Surprisingly, the move from Asia to Russia went very smoothly. I say this as a bit of a "moving expert," having moved just about every year since I first went to boarding school at the age of fourteen, including moves from Baltimore to Singapore, Singapore to Russia, Russia back to the United States, the United States to London, and finally London back to the United States, not to mention moves within Russia and moves within London. So, I was careful when deciding what to bring to Asia and Russia, leaving all the valuable items safely in storage. But three years later, when it came to moving to London and buying the first place of my own, I decided I should have all my favorite things and irreplaceable items like photographs, souvenirs, etc., with me, as I was really making a home there. Of course, life never works out exactly as you plan, and so, not long after, there I was moving again. But this time, I had no fear. It would be an easy move – from the UK to the United States – developed market to developed market. Little did I know the container would get flooded, and I'd lose almost everything. I'll never forget picking through the moldy debris of my precious possessions. My china and ceramics had survived the heat and water, but most of my Persian carpets, Chinese scrolls, Korean wooden chests, Russian boxes – not to mention photos, yearbooks, etc. – had been permanently damaged or destroyed. The lesson for me: while moving is always a hassle, I now know it's also always a risk. So, don't move what you can't imagine living without.

Patricia

I moved back and forth to Russia two times, and each time was a little different. I continued to pack my bags lightly for the freedom and flexibility of the moment. I had no problem finding cheap yet safe apartments, saved a great deal of money, and took advantage of the tax treaty between Russia and the United States. Many countries have such treaties, and finding out about them before making the move is a wise thing to do – 40 to 50 percent of your salary can be taxed in some countries. Russia canceled its tax treaty with the United States during my stint there. Before it ended, I was able to keep almost 100 percent of the income I earned outside the U.S. because (a) I earned less than the U.S. Government limit of $72,000 at the time, and (b) the U.S.-Russia tax treaty allowed nationals living in the other's country to be exempt from local taxes. I say almost 100 percent because, oddly enough, Washington, D.C., required me to continue paying. (And I had to pay double the amount of Social Security and Medicare taxes because as a stringer I was self-employed and had to pay as the employer and the employee.) In the middle of my years as a stringer, the tax treaty was eliminated, and I suddenly owed the Russian Government approximately 40 percent of my salary. You just never know who is going to tax you and when it might change, so be prepared!

After working as a stringer for three years, I was promoted to Moscow Bureau Chief of *BusinessWeek* in 1996. I was thrilled with the promotion and the recognition, and I was given the full expat package with a free apartment, car and driver, and home leave three times a year. One other important benefit was that McGraw-Hill, the owner of *BusinessWeek*, offered a "tax equalization" benefit. In other words, the company paid most of my Russian taxes. I owned an apartment in Washington, D.C., and decided to rent it out rather than selling it. I rented it out furnished, and the first tenant stayed for two years. It worked out well. After that, I needed an agent to help me, as I couldn't manage the place from so far away and with the unreliable communication within Russia. I paid an agent, who found someone who paid less in rent and ended up a deadbeat! Sometimes it's better to do things yourself, but sometimes you can't and therefore must recognize the risks. Another seemingly simple task I couldn't do from so far away was pay my own American bills. The mail to and from Russia was very unreliable and glacially slow. Electronic banking was barely available in the United States in the early nineties because the Internet was in its infancy. I simply trusted my mother to handle my checkbook and pay my bills. It's fascinating to me now as I look back. Today, we take for granted the ease of electronic banking and our ability to access U.S. dollars and local currencies around the world through ATM machines. But the only way I could get my hands on my "paycheck" – I was paid in U.S. dollars directly deposited in my U.S. bank account – was to write a check at the American Express office in Moscow. The ruble was not stable then, and one of the most important non-negotiables for me was to be paid in U.S. dollars. Lucky for me, American Express had an office in central Moscow.

Chapter 5

Being Good to Yourself

To be happy living in a foreign country, you have to take it on its own terms. Don't expect it to be like home. Instead, seek out and enjoy the things that make that country special.
— Patricia, *New York Times*

Living in a foreign country excites the imagination, ignites the adventurous spirit, and inspires you to explore. It can also scare the pants off you. Learning to live in another country is more than simply learning how to get to the office, making yourself understood in the local language, and eating different food. You must learn how to do many new things while also learning how to redo many things that have become second nature. It involves a subtle but important change in your expectations of yourself and others. More importantly, you have to cope with the loss of identity and familiarity and get along without some of the personal perks in your life that provide encouragement, direction, and meaning. We've done it, and so can you.

Focusing on the personal component of the journey, this chapter takes you from arrival through the first year of settling in. We'll prepare you to cope with the inevitable culture shock and explain how best to tap into the local communities to make life a little easier. Your new experiences will be a constant source of stimulation, so we encourage you to revel in them but to be alert because you are in a foreign environment. We'll address the important issue of how best to stay safe while overseas, especially when traveling. Once you've eased into your new lifestyle, you'll probably want to start dating and traveling for pleasure. If so, we've got some smart tips on how to travel, where to shop for what items in various markets around the world, and how to make the most of dating far from home.

You Have Arrived

Although a "look-see" trip gave you a glimpse of your new digs, it's a completely different ballgame once you've landed for good. Most of us approach situations with our eyes and ears wide open. We notice things big and small, and this pays off as we begin to settle in. Without knowing it, many of us who have worked overseas leveraged the traits common to women and successful internationalists that we identified in Chapter 1. Keep these traits in the forefront of your mind, and tap into them to help you adapt to your new environment faster and more successfully. Reiterated here, they are adaptability and flexibility, ability to communicate well, skill at building teams and relationships, patience and persistence, and curiosity and open-mindedness.

One of the many things that can test at least the first four, if not all five, traits is your arrival. Some arrivals go smoothly, with company-arranged transportation, five-star hotel accommodation, and a helpful team in the office. If yours goes this way, the odds of your success are higher, according to HR experts. If your first two weeks are rocky, the rest of your term may suffer. Getting off to a good start requires some on-the-ground assistance, so be sure to have a plan of action to ensure some stability upon arrival. It will make a big difference. It's not necessarily doom and gloom if you get started on the wrong foot, but bad first impressions can make you want to run screaming back home or to the airport!

Making It Real

I arrived at the airport for the first time in Nizhneyvartofsk, Siberia, at 6 a.m. local time and walked out into a shabby, horribly dark, and very cold baggage claim area with stray dogs and broken furniture. It was January, and I'm from Texas! I walked out into the throng of people, and no one was there to meet me. The only person who came up to me was a very drunk, toothless, homeless-looking man. I was a bit tired, and I was getting more and more scared as everyone but he and I left the airport. No more planes were coming in just then, and no one spoke English. The local airline didn't even have an English speaker. I sat on my bag and sobbed for more than an hour, not knowing who to call or even how to. All of my 'type-A-just-do-it' personality melted away, and I morphed into this completely scared, isolated victim. I felt broken and helpless and so tired. Finally, another plane came in. This nice woman approached me and asked if I was Pamela. I told her yes! She couldn't really say much more than that, but she took me to that drunk man and pushed me toward him. He grabbed my bag and walked outside. I was so scared! As it turned out, he had my name, written in Cyrillic letters, on a very thin, small piece of paper. He was my driver! Remember that most things don't go as smoothly as planned, and you will surely laugh about these stories many times over...So have a plan B for the first few days. They will certainly go differently than you anticipated!

– Pamela, The Teagarden Group

You've landed; now you want to get to work. But wait. If possible, do not report for duty the day after you arrive. Negotiate with your supervisor the value of taking one week of personal time out of what will most likely be a multiyear assignment. A few days spent in getting familiar with your surroundings enables you to start your job on the right foot. Not many of us took the time to get settled upon arrival; we then spent months playing catch-up. Once you know where to shop for groceries and work out, know how to use local transportation, and have a friend to call when you're in need, you will be able to jump right into work with some peace of mind. Therefore, we recommend doing six important things during your first week in your new home.

The First Week

- **Nail down your personal must-haves.** For some people a hair salon, a massage therapist, an aerobics class, or a particular brand of tea or coffee may be critical to begin feeling "at home." You might think these things are trivial, and perhaps to some extent they are. But during this high-stress time when so many other things are going to be unfamiliar, you'll find comfort in the small, familiar things and will

107

breathe a sigh of relief with your own personal "basics" in place – those things you probably took for granted back home.

- **Make contact with at least one expat living locally.** Established expats can be a valuable source of information, assistance, and on-the-ground expertise. Chances are that you will already have the names of several, be they people you actually know or, as is more likely, friends of friends. If not, find one either through your office, your alumni association, or a mutual friend. They can answer many "how-to" questions easily and will reduce the stress of having to figure out everything yourself. They will also be the ones to call when you've temporarily had enough or need to share your cultural mishaps.

- **Make sure you have at least one local contact.** There are some things that only a native can help you with, specifically in terms of cultural awareness and understanding. Your office may assign you someone to assist in this capacity. If not, perhaps someone in your office or a friend of an expat can serve as this guide. It's preferable if your local guide has some firsthand understanding of where you're literally coming from.

- **Familiarize yourself with the transportation system.** Whether it's your own car, the subway, or a system of commuter trains or ferries, ride them into, out of, and around your new city. Get relevant schedules and maps. Find out about monthly passes and timetables. Time your commute to the office. Find the best way to get to those local places you'll need to go to most often in the first month or so and how long the trips take.

- **Set up house.** More often than not, your personal goods will not have arrived yet, so you'll have to settle in in phases. Once in your own apartment or house – or even if it's only a hotel room – put away your clothes, put out your photos, and stock the refrigerator with enough food for at least a week, or buy some snacks for your room. Get to know your neighborhood, if possible. Explore the place and learn the amenities and services offered. Make note of anything you don't have but think you might need, like a hair dryer or an iron. Ask your new contacts whether you do need these items; if so, secure them. If you first live in a hotel, make sure to request a few days to set up house when your personal effects arrive.

- **Experience your new home.** Through this first week, and throughout your international adventure, explore your surroundings. Get a feel for the place, and make your first diary entry. Stroll the streets; visit local museums and other tourist attractions; read the local newspaper in a park and watch the people go by. Find a friendly café or tea shop and just hang out.

Your enhanced business acumen will move you up after you've moved abroad – but don't underestimate the value of a good time and lots of personal growth, too. Have fun because you're going to work hard.

Making It Real

One of the best ways to get a real feel for a city is to take a run early in the morning. I love watching cities wake up, as the markets and shopping stalls are set up and the streets slowly fill with people. Once a city starts to hustle with its routine, it's more difficult to look behind the scenes and see how it ticks.

– Barbara, strategy and innovation consultant

Everyone is in the same boat when they arrive. Everyone goes through essentially the same acclimatization process. It can be done. It just takes time. Getting angry and complaining about the situation – regardless of how chaotic it is – will not change a thing.

– Mary, FAA

I can still hear the echo of my footsteps on the lovely marble floors in my Swiss apartment. I had just arrived and there was no furniture to buffer the clatter. I felt quite alone.

– Jackie, Alcon

While queuing for a lunchtime sandwich on my first day in New York, I desperately tried to understand what the assistant was saying. It seemed no one asked for a ham sandwich as we would do in the UK. So many decisions – types of bread, fillings, toppings, sauces – all had to be specified at break-neck speed. As I worked my way up the line, I realized I had no idea what to order! When it was my turn, I said, "same again," referring to the complete stranger in front of me!

– Mary, retired international executive

109

When I first arrived, I remember sitting in a coffee shop watching streams of highly purposeful New Yorkers rushing by with such purpose. They seemed to be on a mission, never pausing to notice what's going on around them.

– Kate, Edelman

My biggest regret is that I didn't keep a detailed diary. I met so many colorful people and saw so many exotic places, it's a shame I don't have a personal, written record of those amazing times. My mother told me to, but I was simply too lazy at night to do it. I preferred to relax and read, since writing was my job. But I suggest that now in the day of the laptop, people write a short entry every night. At the very least, they will be able to remember names and places. And even if they never want to turn it into a book, they will be able to share it with loved ones long after the adventure has ended.

– Patricia, *New York Times*

When I first arrived in Rome, I hopped in a taxi and asked in Italian to go to the Coliseum. The taxi driver took me for a spin around the city, only to drop me off not far from where we started! Even though I spoke Italian, it was obvious I was not from Rome.

– Rosy, former foreign correspondent, *Journal of Commerce*

The First Few Months

Some days you may feel like screaming as you ride the roller coaster of emotions common to people living abroad. In first few months of your assignment, you will probably be thrilled to be there, high on the excitement and the adventure – but at the same time, you may feel pretty stupid as you make what you probably consider silly mistakes. This is just one example of how the many paradoxes you will experience and learn to handle. Naturally, you will assume things are similar to the way they were at home, especially in situations where there appear to be no more than superficial variations. You will have to relearn most of what you take for granted, so your patience, persistence, and ability to be flexible and communicate well will be of paramount importance. In the beginning, your uncertainty will likely increase. This happens because the more you learn, the more you realize you don't know what you're doing, resulting in increasing discomfort and uncertainty. You're operating without a net, and suddenly your abundance of confidence begins to wane. Do not despair. You're experiencing culture shock.

Culture shock is generally defined as the confusion, disorientation, and emotional upheaval that inevitably results from finding yourself immersed in a new culture. It consists of three phases. In the first, the honeymoon phase, everything is absolutely grand. Next, fabulous turns to a period of frustration, depression, and confusion that is often triggered by an event involving minor cultural differences. All usually ends well as the recovery phase, characterized by increased adjustment and satisfaction, rounds out the experience. You will experience culture shock, and you must go through it yourself to understand it. It's helpful, therefore, to read books about culture shock and talk to others who have undergone it and emerged from it.

Culture Shock Literature

Culture shock can manifest itself in many different ways, and the topic has spawned a small subindustry within travel guides. Our favorite is the *Culture Shock!* series published by Graphic Arts Center Publishing Industry, in Portland, Oregon. At this writing, there were hundreds of these books, covering more than a hundred countries and dozens of cities and updated every few years or so. The pages offer information designed to help the traveler adjust to her new environs. These books provide the history, describe the people, explain the workings of key institutions, and offer clues on how the locals will deal with you and how you can deal with them. Although nothing beats experience, advance preparation can help. Such books can also help you understand what is going on after you've experienced it.

Making It Real

One way to prepare for culture shock is to try to understand the customs, anticipate what you won't like, and then figure out how you'll deal with it. A good poker face also comes in handy!

– **Nancy, Handelsbanken**

It wasn't until my son was two years old that I learned that for Brits, "pants" are what Americans call "underwear" and "trousers" are the outer garment covering waist to ankles. I learned this difference when I misused the word "pants," and someone actually pulled her "pants" out of her waistband to show me the error of my ways. I thought back to the countless number of times I used "pants" incorrectly over the past three years! I laughed at myself – and still do when I think of it.

– **Nancy, Columbia University**

In the United States, "shagging" is a type of Southern dance. So when a favorite "shagging" song came on the jukebox in a bar in Singapore, I told my British clients about how we used to shag all the time in college, how I loved it, and how I shagged anytime I could. After I finished and noticed the looks on their faces, someone politely told me that the British definition of "shag" was "to have sex." Needless to say I was utterly mortified!

– **Perry, coauthor and Kraft Foods, Inc.**

I traveled with a friend to a country in the former Soviet Union where we were invited to be guests in the home of a young local family. The family's apartment had the typical Soviet two-room bathroom where, next to each other, you have a door to go through to use a toilet (a room as small as a closet), and another door to use the bathtub and sink. My friend didn't see the second door, so when he went into the bathtub/sink room, he thought he was supposed to urinate in the tub (since there was no toilet). He thought to himself "this is how people do things here," so he started doing his thing into the tub. Then, the young wife of the family entered the room to wash her hands and saw my friend standing, doing his thing. She thought "this is how they do things over there" and was of course horrified!

– **Nancy, Handelsbanken**

I went to Singapore as a size 14-16 – not an Asian size at all. Sometimes I would walk into the local Singapore dress designer shops and look at their selection. The sales staff was very quick to point out, "We have nothing for you" or "You are King Kong size." The first time it happened to me, I was stunned. But after I admitted it to my friends, they owned up that it happened to them as well, and they were sizes 8s and 10s. What we took as

112

offensive was really the sales people trying to be helpful and moving us along.

— **Mary, FAA**

After being in Russia a few months, I learned one day that I would have no hot water for a month. This was on top of learning the day before that my e-mail service was cut off because the company demanded $2,000 for past service and $500 per month for future service. I received no notice that I was being cut off. It was so frustrating.

— **Karin, The Nature Conservancy**

When I first arrived in Switzerland, I spoke French but by no means flawlessly. One day in the company cafeteria I was trying to ask one of the female staff whether the salad bar items had preservatives in them. As I did this, she couldn't help herself from laughing out loud because the word I used in French meant "condom" not preservative!

— **Jackie, Alcon**

In the first two weeks of our stay in Japan, my husband and I went on a "company outing" to a Japanese onsen (outdoor natural hot spring bath in a mountain setting). I came equipped with my one-piece swim suit and full-length beach towel. I soon realized that swim suits were not worn, and the towels used are roughly the size of a hand towel. Although the men and women had separate facilities, I was shocked and embarrassed at first, especially being the only Western woman. I soon discovered that the whole experience was extremely discreet, very comfortable, and relaxing. Japanese hot springs are a real treat!

— **Mary, Motorola**

Shortly after I arrived in Singapore, I had a driver pick me up at my home in the evening to take me to the airport. The driver was quite talkative and kept asking me questions about my apartment, how much I paid for it, and then he asked me about my husband. I said I didn't have one, and he was quiet for a few minutes and kept looking at me in the rear-view mirror. Finally he said, "You not so ugly, la, how come you don't have a husband?"!

— **Sheila, Barclays Bank**

I think Europeans tend to be wonderfully at ease with who they are but infuriatingly apathetic, whereas Americans tend to be fired up with the 'land of opportunity' belief that they can do anything, but are so self-conscious. The relationship is like a middle-aged parent and an adolescent child.

– **Kate, Edelman**

Settling In

You feel strange, as if you don't belong, because you are foreign. Many cultures just don't let outsiders into the inner circle right away. The sense of distrust and suspicion on their parts, combined with your own sense of uncertainty, creates an uncomfortable atmosphere. It takes effort and energy to keep an open mind because it is so easy to slip into criticism of the local culture and make prejudicial comparisons with your own. Different does not equal bad. Newcomers to a culture must work hard at keeping their natural ethnocentrism under control. Your happiness, and therefore your success, depend on your ability to appreciate your new home culture for what it is, as opposed to what it is not. Embrace it!

One way to begin adapting to your new environment is to build relationships with local friends – people who can be your cultural guides and who are willing to answer your questions. You will find that if you demonstrate a genuine interest in and respect for their culture, most nationals are more than happy to explain various aspects of it to you. If you focus on slowly building relationships with everyone you encounter – from your administrative assistant to your apartment complex manager – you will begin to integrate.

The Value of the Expat Community

Tapping into the resources of an established expat community might prove to be one of the best ways of easing into another culture. If you involve yourself in an established network of similar people, you will find new friends and be able to get involved in activities that you might never get around to on your own. This community will help you settle in faster and make things feel a little more like home. In some cities, there are established clubs for English-speaking Westerners. It seems the more exotic the culture, the more cohesive and close-knit the expat community. In some cities, they are a mixture of transient business folks and established local residents who are intent on maintaining their own culture. Whether official or unofficial, these compatriots offer valuable information on the basics of setting up house, securing good medical attention, identifying the most appropriate schools, finding your favorite food items, and the like. They provide a sense of comfort and familiarity to families, especially those with children. In addition, they also offer easy friendships when you need companionship. Sometimes you just need someone who speaks a familiar language and who understands where you're coming from.

Making It Real

I was surprised at the number of people who, when they found out I was moving to Russia, knew someone living there and were keen to put me in touch. In hindsight, one of the smartest things I did – and I did it as a fluke – was make a list of these Moscow contacts. I figured I'd probably never do anything with it, but I might as well take it along. As I settled in, so too did the reality of not knowing anyone; I called one of the names on the list one afternoon. The guy invited me to an opening of a new pub that night – The Moosehead – where I ended up meeting lots of people. I never did call anyone else on the list, as the contacts made on that night grew into a huge network. Interestingly, I eventually met all of the people on the list during my four years there.

– Kimberly, The Radiate Group

It's usually not very hard to tap into the expat community. There are almost always a few bars where English-speakers congregate – often Irish bars! In many countries there are Brits who have formed a branch of the Hash House Harriers – a running and drinking club. This group is a great way to see the sights (they do a different route every time) and make friends.

– Patricia, *New York Times*

For all its positive benefits, the expat community can also hinder your ability to integrate. It can provide too much comfort and familiarity, and if you let it, it can almost completely insulate you from local society, thus retarding your ability to integrate with your new colleagues and preventing you from experiencing those things that make living overseas such an adventure. Use the expat community for the connections, the network, and a periodic dose of familiarity, but do not make it your dominant or sole social circle. Everything is best when taken in moderation.

Some days you'll think you could live there forever. Other days you'll wish your assignment was over. These feelings are normal and part of the process of integration. You will eventually settle into a pattern that works for you as you become more grounded. You should not expect to feel comfortable in your new culture until late in the first year. But you will get there.

Enjoying the Experience and Traveling

Have fun! Living in a new country brings with it the opportunity to explore. Enjoy all the wonderful aspects of your surroundings. Be a tourist, whether you do so within the greater confines of your city, country, or beyond. Living in another part of the world provides limitless possibilities for exploration and adventure. There is so much to see, so little time. Take advantage of it while you're there; you might not get the opportunity again. Don't work so hard that you leave your posting without having seen the country. Think of it as treating yourself, as well as expanding your mind.

Making It Real

I often went to the ballet and the opera and will never forget the time I saw the Nutcracker at Christmas time at a theater inside the Kremlin walls. The last scene was designed to look as if the dancers were walking through the Kremlin Gates as soft snow fell down on them. When we exited the theater, we crossed the same bridge during a light snowfall. It was magical.

— **Patricia,** *New York Times*

An overseas assignment usually involves a lot of travel, whether within your base country itself or in the encompassing region. Whenever you travel, try to take an extra day to explore the local life, restaurants, and shopping. These little excursions aren't all a boondoggle. They actually help bring you a step closer to understanding the cultures and people you are doing business with.

— **Barbara, strategy and innovation consultant**

I wanted to put some effort into improving my Russian, and so, rather than sitting in Moscow for several weeks on an intensive

116

language programme, I found a tutor who was available to travel with me. We spent six weeks travelling through Central Asia and the Caucasus, speaking virtually no English. This atypical immersion did the trick, as I was forced to do everything in Russian – ask directions, order food, hitchhike (our predominant mode of transport). Part of the value of living and working abroad is not only having the opportunity to do things you otherwise would not have had, but also in developing the ability to recognise the many options that exist.

– Kimberly, The Radiate Group

It's fun to keep track of the spas you've visited around the world. My favorite is in Jordan. After five months in Iraq, I spent time at the famous Sanctuary Spa in the Movenpick Hotel by the Dead Sea. I had five body treatments in two days – and lugged enough salt and mud back home to start my own spa! Actually my purchases, which totaled more than a car payment, made great gifts.

– Joanne, USAID

One of the most important things I learned is the importance of "the little things" we carry with us each day. Yes, personal belongings make life nicer and to some extent easier, but I don't remember the outfit I wore ten years ago. I do remember the little girl in the bright red skirt and crisp white blouse who came with her class to dance for my colleagues and me in a city in Ecuador. She twirled and smiled into the night.

– Karin, The Nature Conservancy

As a woman who has traveled to nearly eighty countries, I have some advice: Never underestimate the value of a great pair of black pants! All you need is a few colorful blazers and no one will realize that you've worn the same pants three times on one trip. Once, while visiting seven East European cities in three weeks, I made the mistake of putting all my "tops" in one suitcase and all my "bottoms" in another. Of course, one suitcase didn't arrive until I was in the third country on the trip. I never made that mistake again!

– Joanne, USAID

Packing Wisely to Travel Well

- When in doubt, leave it out. Don't over-pack.

- If bringing more than one suitcase, pack complete outfits together.

- Be able to carry or wheel your own luggage.

- Bring a carry-on containing your essentials and one complete outfit.

- Save room for souvenirs.

- Bring a guidebook and/or fiction based in the city or country.

- Carry a large scarf or Pashmina shawl for over-air-conditioned conference rooms and planes or to use as a head scarf in Muslim countries.

- Bring flat, comfortable shoes.

- Pack workout gear that is modest and not revealing or too tight-fitting.

Shop the World

One of the best things about global travel is the shopping. Every country has its own specialties, such as gold in the Middle East, leather in Argentina or Italy, watches in Hong Kong, and local art in most countries. It is great fun (and at times a bit frustrating) to shop in a market unlike your own. The sights, the sounds, the textures – the entire experience is different in some fashion or another, including the transaction itself. Whether you're buying as an investment or for the sheer pleasure of acquiring interesting trinkets, you will most likely be taken a little advantage of. Those who insist they "got the best" of a local merchant are either fooling themselves or have involved a local to negotiate/buy for them. But if you like what you've got and feel you paid a fair price, there's no reason to get angry or frustrated or feel insulted. Half the fun is negotiating – at least, that's the position most merchants around the world seem to take. The following are some tips on what to buy from those who've shopped the world over ... with a few standing pieces of advice:

1. Know the quality and value (at least to you) of what you are buying before you purchase.

2. Keep in mind that bargaining in many parts of the world includes drinking tea or coffee with the merchants – and not paying the first price offered.

3. Use cash for better bargaining power, and prepare a quick cheat sheet of equivalent values in increments, such as 50 worth of the local currency (or be able to mentally calculate currency conversions quickly) so you don't overpay in the heat of the deal.

4. Know the laws pertaining to the nature and quantity of merchandise that you are allowed to leave the country with, especially those on removing antiques and objects of historic or cultural importance.

Above all, *enjoy yourself*, for shopping around the world is truly one of the global woman's best perks! There are no international guidebooks on what to buy where, and circumstances, prices, and quality can change rapidly, so we've put together an unofficial list of great global buys! The following are some of the highlights:

- Carpets in Eastern Europe, Central Asia, the Middle East, and India
- Textiles in Vietnam, Cambodia, Thailand, Italy, India, and Eastern Europe
- Rubies and sapphires in Burma, emeralds in Brazil, diamonds in Belgium or Holland, pearls in China
- Silver in India, Thailand, Vietnam, Cambodia, and Morocco
- Crystal or glassware in Eastern Europe, Italy, and Sweden
- China or porcelain in Taiwan, Japan, and Korea
- Electronics and software in the United States
- Cashmere in Nepal and Mongolia
- Purses, luggage, silk, and tons of inexpensive items you didn't think you needed but couldn't live without in China
- Tailored clothes in Hong Kong, but not a three-day turnaround – go to a legitimate tailor who will take 10-14 days to make your clothes; they'll last a lifetime and look like Chanel…or Dior…or Moschino
- Wines in South Africa, New Zealand, Australia, Chile, Argentina, Italy, France, and California, USA

Making It Real

You rarely regret what you buy, but you'll remember forever what you let slip by.

– Joanne, USAID

I became friends with Elena, a sculptor, who had artists on both sides of her family tree. Her mother made prints of Bolshoi ballerinas. Her father fulfilled his military duty in World War II by painting battle scenes for the Soviet Army. Her maternal grandfather was a famous graphic artist. Elena and her cousins treated me like family, inviting me often to their apartments and vacation houses, which were filled with works of art. When it came time to leave Russia, I bought a half dozen of her grandfather's paintings and prints. Although many people bought contemporary artists, I wanted to preserve the personal and historical connection to my friends. I also came home with a sculpture of myself made by Elena and Constructivist-style prints of scenes from the Bolshevik Revolution. Since antiquities – anything created before 1930 – are not allowed out of the country, a representative from the Russian Ministry of Culture came to inspect and stamp my art work before I could take it home.

– Patricia, *New York Times*

Safety

As a woman living overseas you must be careful about your safety. Don't take chances. Be attentive. We've already mentioned that other cultures will have impressions of "what women are like" from your part of the world. Whether they are accurate or not, you will need to know those perceptions and anticipate them. Your safety could be at risk. Many of the tips on traveling safely internationally are similar to those for safe traveling domestically. We've included them here under the heading "traveling safely" for three reasons: (1) living overseas can be considered a type of travel because you are outside your home country, (2) many international positions include travel, (3) personal travel requires the same attention that business travel does. However, there are a few twists on the norm.

Traveling Safely

- Acknowledge that, in some countries, women do not have equal legal rights as men.

120

- Find out from your embassy or consult a specialty firm like Control Risk to determine which countries/cities are noted as dangerous or those with different laws for women.

- Don't be caught by surprise; be aware of your surroundings at all times.

- Don't take anything for granted. Err on the side of caution when it comes to strangers.

- Stay in company-approved business hotels; make sure your staff in your office knows where you are going, where you will be staying, and with whom you're meeting.

- Always have cash hidden on your person.

- Be cautious of your attire, including appropriate clothes and amount of jewelry.

- Lock your passport in your hotel safe. If there isn't one or you don't think it is secure, keep your passport on your person at all times, i.e., not in a purse or bag.

- Know the local laws and abide by them.

- Don't arrive late at night at a place you either do not know or suspect is dangerous.

- Do not let any hotel front desk announce your room number aloud. If they do, insist they give you another.

- Request rooms near the elevator and not at the end of long hallways. Reserve rooms on the first to seventh floor for evacuation safety. Street-level floors can be vulnerable.

- Always use the front entrance to your hotel.

- Don't walk alone at night unless it's necessary.

- Use company-sponsored cars or approved taxi companies.

- If you are driving, be sure to have your car serviced before you go or rent from a reputable car company. Have a flashlight, water, and maps that indicate where the police stations and hospitals are located.

- Keep your cell phone charged, taking advantage of short stops to plug in.

Appreciate Political Dynamics Affecting International Business

Political tension sometimes spills over into the business world. It pays to be smart and attentive when it comes to strife, tension, and hostility among particular countries, cultures, or religions. As a globetrotting citizen, you are an unofficial ambassador for your home country and should act in a dignified way. This can be especially critical during times of military operations, internal tensions, or even the opening up of new markets, such as during the Cold War in Russia or after the Cultural Revolution in China. At the time of this writing, there is tension between the West and many Muslim nations. But global commerce continues, and therefore, it is prudent to understand the basics of doing business with one another. As we've advised in previous chapters, you must do your homework for your personal and professional best interests. Here are a few tips that some of our friends who are both Muslim doing business in the West and vice versa have suggested. They are not meant to be comprehensive; we simply want to shed a little light on the differences.

For **Western women traveling to Muslim countries, understand that the role of women is different** – not better or worse but different. In some Muslim countries, women do not have the same legal rights as men, nor do they have the same business responsibilities. Do not judge, condemn, or compare your own culture in a more favorable light (at least not publicly, do whatever you feel in private). On a personal level, **take care in how you dress**. Wear pants and long-sleeved, long shirts (or long loose skirts that don't show the body's contours), and of course, it is very important to cover cleavage and midriff. Carry a scarf with you at all times and **cover your head as appropriate**. **Do not flirt**; be careful in your interactions with men so as not to be misinterpreted. Know that Muslim cultures exist around the world, not only in the Middle East, but throughout Africa, Eastern Europe, and Asia. Just as the West and Asia cannot be viewed through one cultural lens, nor can Islamic cultures. Do your research, make sure you have a local guide, and follow the local customs as much as you can out of respect for your business partner. Being invited to a Muslim's home with a banquet prepared and fit for a king is a form of high regard and a means for developing the important personal relationships. You must follow a certain protocol; ask your host for advice.

122

For **Muslim women traveling to the West**, especially the United States, know that **business relationships are generally segregated from personal ones**. Do not be offended if you are not invited to their homes, do not get to know them personally, or learn very little about their lives outside the office. However, **Americans can be very social and easygoing**, asking you seemingly personal questions such as how you met your husband, how many children you have, or what activities you like to do on the weekends. This is all part of casual, get-to-know-you chatting before business begins. Compared to Europe, the **United States is a more conservative and religious culture** in general, though there certainly are exceptions. Life as depicted by American TV series or films constitutes fictional portrayals far from the realities of daily American life. The **woman's role in society can be prominent in business culture**; Westerners are proud of the "equality" of the sexes. Women dress in business attire, and a display of bare skin, uncovered heads, and makeup are considered acceptable. Finally, you should be aware that there exist anti-Muslim sentiments since 9/11, and related feelings of pain, sorrow, and anger continue in the United States. But most likely these will not be directed at you personally.

We all have preconceived notions of people of other cultures; Muslims and Westerners are no exception. Especially in today's times, both need to be patient and to work carefully and diligently to show the real culture to each other. You will need to be able to explain aspects of your backgrounds, your religion, and your culture, including the roles of men and women, the Hijab (veil) for Muslims, and the lack of religion in many parts of business and daily life for some Westerners. An understanding of each other will be critical to being able to do business successfully and may even become channels to help push forward understanding across their respective cultures.

Sexual Misinterpretation

Almost every woman we've spoken to about being overseas has a story about being "hit on" or, to put it more politely, receiving amorous advances. There are many reasons why, such as that men think that since you are a strong confident woman, you don't have a man and so you may want/need sex. Some misinterpret your strength as a sexual advance, finding independent self-assured women appealing. Some may want to take advantage of the fact that you are in a foreign land and may not know how to call for help. Sometimes it's culturally acceptable to have affairs and lovers, so your coworkers or clients will think that you are game. Whatever the reason, you can almost certainly count on it happening to you. Here are a few stories from our surveyed women, which – for obvious reasons – we've left anonymous this time. In most of these circumstances, the women firmly but politely declined the advances or left the scene. Your surprise, disgust, or overreaction may amuse the man making the advance. Keep your safety first and foremost, and if you don't think you can handle the situation by yourself, call for help. Keep in mind that wearing a wedding band does not keep these men at bay – in fact, it sometimes invites them in.

One of my coworkers came on to me at a meeting. I told him I was married, and he said, 'That's good, so am I. It makes it less complicated, no?'

I had wrapped up a contract with a client in Malaysia, and he asked me for tea in the hotel lobby. I accepted, we talked, and then he asked if I was ready to go to his room. I stuttered and asked what did he mean? He said that he assumed, naturally, since I was an American consultant that I was part of the package, for why else would he pay $350 an hour for my time?

I was traveling with a senior official of a foreign government. When we checked into the hotel, he had the porter 'accidentally' take my suitcase to his room. He called to tell me of the mistake, and when I knocked, I saw that my bags were on the other side of the room. Naively, I accepted his polite assertion that it was fine for me to come in and get my bags quickly. He locked the door as soon as I was in and chased me around the room! If it hadn't been for his aide, who had both a key and familiarity with his boss's modus operandi, I could have suffered more than embarrassment.

Once I was on a train in Japan when a man sat across from me with a briefcase on his lap. He closed his eyes, and I thought he fell asleep ... until his briefcase started going up and down. He was masturbating right in front of me!

On one of my first trips to Dubai, I was walking and nine different cars stopped and men told me to get in. Even though I was wearing a business suit, they thought I was a prostitute.

It takes a lot to get used to male strangers touching you without your permission. Part of it is cultural. Part of it is just rude. But it happens, and you have to find your own way of dealing with it, but without fuss.

Many times men in Western countries would assume I was 'easy' and would do what they said because I came from what was perceived as a 'submissive' culture for women.

Dating

There are guides to help you learn the language, learn to shop, and learn to get around, but not much published material that can really help you with cross-cultural dating. That you have to learn on your own. Dating overseas is not like dating someone from your home country, in your home country. Subtleties and nuances in the culture feel very different when they are being exhibited by your date. Being friends just isn't the same. It can be both fun and frustrating. Unless you want to be alone while you are living overseas, singles will likely have to learn how to navigate the high-stakes world of cross-cultural dating.

Making It Real

Foreign women are a novelty to men in some cultures. I know many women who had no problems finding dates wherever they moved. But stepping it up a notch to a cross-cultural marriage was a totally different concept. There's a world of difference between a foreign girlfriend and a foreign wife. Some people just can't go there.

– Pam, published author

I met my husband while working in New York – a perfect gentleman from the Midwest. He was so polite that I didn't realize he was hitting on me for some months.

– Kate, Edelman

125

Whether it is expat to expat or expat to local, cross-cultural dating has all the normal challenges of dating – plus a whole lot more. During the ten years I lived abroad, I dated plenty of men, and I had my fair share of interesting and enlightening experiences. From the private clubs only Russians could visit to the Chinese New Year holiday rituals you can only experience in a Chinese home, I had a chance to see other cultures on a whole different level. Not all were experiences I'd care to repeat, but they did bring a whole new level of international understanding. And they couldn't have been all bad, as I turned around and married a foreigner upon returning to the United States – effectively signing me up for cross-cultural intimacy for life!

– Perry, coauthor and Kraft Foods, Inc.

Most New York men have a totally different concept of "chatting up" than London men. New Yorkers seem to have a checklist of questions that you have to pass before they judge if you are worth spending any time with. Some sound unbelievably blunt, like "how much do you make," "what religion are you," and "where did your father go to school." British men tend to try to make you laugh – but they can also forget to ask your name!

– Kate, Edelman

Fairy tales can come true; here's my story: Girl meets boy while living in Singapore. Girl and boy fall in love. After a year together, girl confronts boy and finds out that he will not marry out of his culture. Girl breaks up with boy and leaves country. A year later, boy shows up on girl's doorstep in New York, and they get married. Boy's father disowns him. Boy and girl have a little girl of their own. This little girl is the first girl born in boy's father's family in more than 60 years. Little girl becomes princess and the original girl becomes a queen in the family's household. Happy ending!

– Pam, published author

If you ever walk alone in the streets of Rome, especially at night, you will very likely find yourself suddenly escorted by numerous men asking why you are alone. They will offer to personally show you their glorious city! I have heard many women say that when you are in Rome, you feel like a woman.

– Rosy, former foreign correspondent, *Journal of Commerce*

If you think of your time abroad as a personal as well as professional learning experience, you'll do just fine. Here are personal stories from three of our six women who came to terms with one aspect or another of the ambient culture during their time abroad.

The Journey Continues

Patricia

In the winter of 1996-97 I traveled to Vorkhuta, a coal mining town north of the Arctic Circle, with colleagues. We had dinner at the foreman's house that night. He called his wife and said he was bringing home guests. She and her girlfriend, who had done all the cooking on short notice, were made to eat in the kitchen while we were all in the living room – all men except for me. I felt uncomfortable because it seemed like he was treating his wife like a servant. At the dinner, the foreman made several comments that American women were not like Russian women, that Americans were "hard" and "unfeminine." I had heard such things before, and I could usually let them pass, but he kept repeating it. Finally, I went into the kitchen to get away, and to thank his wife for the meal. She and her friend told me that I didn't fit their image of American women – which they got from TV! I can't remember exactly what shows were aired there at the time, but since most were soaps operas or shows like *Dynasty* and *Dallas*, they thought American women were all rich and glamorous! All this criticism (and vodka) finally got to me, and I started crying. Then the women themselves said, "See, American women are soft, too!" That got me even madder! It sure was a night of cultural contrasts. The place was remote, far even from Moscow, and so I could understand where they were coming from. But it was a bit hard to take. I knew the man loved his wife and that wives stay behind the scenes in business situations. But sometimes the way women were treated made me angry.

Jackie

I never would have imagined myself carrying US$25,000 in cash in my briefcase to Russia to do a deal and then being the only one of my group (the colleagues with whom I was traveling were all male) to be stopped at the border and searched! My two colleagues strolled right through customs at the border of an industrial town in a region far from Moscow. I was following right behind them when a customs officer tapped me on the shoulder, spoke to me in Russian, and motioned me off to the side to a counter, where he took my briefcase. A couple of his fellow officers came over, and they proceeded to open my briefcase and take out the contents, including the $25,000, busily conversing in Russian. I was starting to get nervous when I remembered that we could bring *in* all the hard currency we wanted – it was taking it *out* that could be a problem. So my anxiety turned to annoyance and then to amusement as I spotted my colleagues through a window, standing outside smoking, peering through the window, and laughing at me. The customs officers pulled out a bunch of forms and duly recorded every bill that I had in my briefcase, added them up, had me sign the forms and then repacked everything and sent me on my way. I decided that they either didn't have enough to do that day or just wanted to make a woman wait for a little while at the border.

That day was only surpassed by the night's dinner complete with traditional Russian fare, including dancing girls and lots of vodka. We may laugh at these anecdotes, but you can learn a lot from them, such as what it takes to form and solidify relationships. You learn about customs, norms, and local people's lives. You can learn what it takes to get a deal done and that what may be viewed as a bit strange in another country may just be "the way it is here."

Stacie

During the course of our three years in Hong Kong, we managed to visit most every country in the region. We celebrated anniversaries and birthdays in exotic destinations such as Sri Lanka, New Zealand, and Tibet – places that I doubt we would have visited had we not been regional residents. I was able to fulfill a personal dream as we took advantage of long weekends, business trips, and vacations to explore the rich history, natural beauty, and colorful cultures of Asia. Although we enjoyed some glorious resorts and were pampered at a few five-star hotels, we also frequently chose to get out and explore the cities, comb the countryside, and experience the heart and soul of a place. Many friends and family members also took advantage of our exotic address and vacationed in Asia; we were able to share some of the local flavor with both of our mothers and my sister and brother, as we served as guides and fellow tourists in Hong Kong and beyond.

Luckily for us, Hong Kong is a regional airline hub, which made bargain tickets and package deals easy to come by. We spent weekends at the beach in Saipan, Panang, and Cebu, and skied in Korea, which has the perk of natural hot springs that serve as an outdoor après-ski hot tub. Using Bali as a starting point, we hopped eastward through the Lesser Sunda Islands, ending up on Komodo, home of the famous dragons – several of which even slept under our cabin. We climbed through the Cu Chi tunnels on the outskirts of Saigon and heard "the other side of the story" as told by our former Viet Cong guide. After spinning the prayer wheels while circling the Potala, we shared tea with Tibetans and gazed at the Dalai Lama's deserted palace. We took to the streets like locals as we bicycled through several cities in China, including Tianjin, where my father was stationed as a U.S. Marine in the late 1940s – and a place I felt compelled to visit. We marveled at the exquisite textiles, porcelain, and other works of art now housed in the National Palace Museum in Tai Pei, Taiwan, but formerly part of the beauty and grandeur of the now empty Forbidden City in Beijing. My husband watched as I bungee-jumped off the Kawarau Suspension Bridge near Queenstown, and we swam with wild dolphins at dawn in Kaikoura, New Zealand.

Therefore, my most ardent piece of advice to anyone living overseas is this: *travel* as frequently as possible and to the most exotic locales. It expands the mind. Besides, you will really need the break after all the long hours you will be putting in. I know how hard it can be to pull yourself away from the responsibilities of your job, but you owe it to yourself and your employer. You'll also learn a lot about yourself and the big, wide world around you.

Chapter 6

The First Year On the Job: Surviving and Delivering

There are more similarities than differences to doing business in different countries, but it's important to understand the nuances. There is an art to managing subtleties, and I believe I mastered it. In doing so, it helped me deliver in demanding roles, increase my knowledge of cultural differences, and boost my own self-confidence. My career truly took off after I went overseas.

— Anna, former BP executive

Your first year on the ground is critical. Do everything you can to make the most of your time abroad. Doing the best job you can in a climate of unknowns will challenge you to figure out how best *you* can succeed in your specific circumstances. Learning to work in another country takes a great deal of energy and commitment. Everyone tells a slightly different story on how they made it work. It will depend in large part on your background, industry, and environment. However, what *is* common to all are the three professional stages we go through as part of the overseas assignment. The next three chapters will cover how to make the most of your professional experience on the ground in your new location and upon your return home or to HQ. The timeframes given below are intended only as guideposts, not as hard-and-fast rules, since everyone moves at her own pace.

1. **Surviving and delivering.** During the first six to nine months, you are going to be most concerned with just doing the job you were

hired to do. This involves figuring out what you need to do, how you're going to get it done, and then making it happen.

2. **Expanding and marketing**. During the next six to twenty-four months, you will want to distinguish yourself, showcase your success, and market your capabilities while growing your role and expanding your responsibilities.

3. **Ensuring a Successful Return**. Whether it's after three or ten years abroad, once you decide to return to your home market, you will need to make the most of your experience – both professionally and personally.

In this chapter, we'll discuss the first step: survive and deliver. We'll cover the subsequent two stages in Chapters 7 and 8, respectively.

Surviving and Delivering

If you're going to make it past the first year, you'll need to prove quickly that you've got what it takes. Once you've landed, HQ will check in with you periodically, but the local environment is the one you must conquer. The local team generally gives you a few months – let's say a hundred days – to start delivering. During that time you will generally be granted some benefit of the doubt. But after that, you must demonstrate that you are capable, no matter how junior or senior you are, or you will lose the respect you seek and the trust you need from your colleagues on the ground. If you succeed quickly, your reputation will grow. If you don't, overcoming a lackluster first impression will be a monumental challenge.

One of the best ways to ensure success is to listen carefully and figure out what's going on and why. Then you can begin to make things happen, whether it is instituting changes, putting systems in place to solve problems, or addressing business-specific needs. Pay attention the first few months, and carefully consider situations before acting. It may be difficult for go-getters like you to do, but resist the temptation to jump in and do it "your way." Listen.

Making It Real

When I arrived to run the manufacturing operation in Mechelen, Belgium, I felt like an alien. Out of the 350, almost all-male workforce, I was the lone American — and female. It was the first time in my life when I doubted my own ability. I went because I strongly believe that to get to the very top, you have to put yourself in a position at least once where you have a 50/50 chance of failure. I knew I had to figure out how to work smartly or I would fail. I had very sweaty palms and many a sleepless night!

– Diane, DuPont

I was invited to an off-site lunch (for a former employer) my first Friday working in Surrey, England. I was surprised to see that we were pulling up to a traditional "old English pub." Once inside all of my colleagues ordered pints of beer. I followed suit. Then they ordered another along with lunch — which was more like a full-course dinner with meat, potatoes, etc. The meal lasted more than two hours, and I came to learn that this was standard practice for Friday afternoons. We headed back to the office in the late afternoon. I had many more of these Friday excursions, and although it was difficult for me as an American to have such a large and relaxing afternoon meal (I really wanted to be working and getting things done back at the office), I came to realize how important this gathering was to the overall sense of team and relationship-building.

– Gretchen, Deloitte Services LP

I arrived in Hong Kong one year before the handover of the territory to China. Hong Kong people had gone through a rough time in the previous six or seven years. They suffered disbelief at first, but then came to accept that Britain was not going to give them all passports, and therefore, they would become Chinese citizens on July 1, 1997. Tension and distrust were thick in the air, but no one ever mentioned a word — at least not at first. Although my team was warm and welcoming, they saw me as a teacher, someone from whom they could learn new skills — skills that would be an added bonus to their resumes during this time of uncertainty. I made it a point to transfer as much knowledge to them as I could, taking pains to review and share in detail, not just give orders. They absorbed like sponges and gave back to me 100 percent all the time. Had I not realized this very early on, I would not have been nearly as successful as I was.

– Stacie, coauthor and consultant

As a journalist I had to deliver good stories to be successful. And in a place that was undergoing as much change as Russia was during the 1990s, good stories popped up as quickly as mushrooms after a rainstorm. In Russia, it didn't take long for me to fulfill that dream – from stories about fledgling businesses created as a result of Gorbachev's perestroika reforms to the first time people felt free to express their opinions in newspapers or letters or TV news shows without fearing that they would be sent to jail or worse. I wrote the first draft of history, fulfilling most journalists' dreams.

–**Patricia,** *New York Times*

Getting Started

If you are like most of us, you will look back on those first few months and laugh at yourself, your naiveté, and your cultural bungling. Making mistakes is natural when you are operating in a foreign environment. Moreover, you'll be operating at warp speed as you try to settle in, get the lay of the land, and start making things happen. There won't be enough hours in the day to resolve the numerous paradoxes or complex problems you'll encounter while working abroad. But you'll have to do so anyway. After you're a few months into the groove – perhaps by the end of the first year – you'll be wiser to the local ways. You'll come to realize that many of the difficulties you encounter are due to who you are – not who your new compatriots are. But this new life is not what you're used to, and it's imperative to keep this point in mind.

In fact, we recommend that you spend a small amount of time, right in the beginning, figuring out the best way for you to keep improving. Once you get into the groove, the pace runs at breakneck speed, so we've devised a list of practical tenets, which we call "Making the Most It Maxims." It is critical that you understand them as you begin the journey. We then recommend that you put this list somewhere where you will read it every morning before you start your day. You can tape it to your bathroom mirror or turn it into a book mark to slip into the magazine, newspaper, or book you are currently reading. Becoming familiar with each maxim will make it easier for you to accept that you are who you are, while keeping front and center the importance of understanding your new environment as quickly and effectively as you can. You want to do more than just get by; you want to be as successful as you can be.

"Making the Most of It" Maxims

1. **Remember that you are the guest and therefore may need to modify your style.**
2. **Figure out what the cultural norms are in social and business environments.**
3. **Accept that paradoxes are part and parcel of the international adventure.**
4. **Don't be too hard on yourself when you make mistakes.**
5. **Draw on your female management style.**
6. **Keep a positive attitude.**

First, succeeding abroad usually depends on effectively adapting your behavior to coincide with local norms. Is there something in your style that you should tone down or amplify? What aspects of your character or traits will enable you to make every new impression a positive one? First impressions matter, and you will be creating lots of them. To make sure your substance shines through, every day ask yourself who you'll be meeting, what they are like, and whether there is something you can and should do to enhance the interaction.

Second, things are not always as they seem, look, or even sound. Be cautious, take note, and if something happens that seems strange or contradictory to you, ask one of your local guides. You must learn the written and unwritten rules, which may vary by industry, hierarchy, and culture. Pay attention, ask questions, and figure out how things are done in your new environment. Reading books on culture shock can advance your knowledge in this area. An ounce of preventive embarrassment could save you pounds of mortification.

Third, as we'll explore later in this chapter, cross-cultural life presents a bounty of situations in which you will find yourself facing apparently contradictory positions. These paradoxes can inhibit your ability to perform your job well if you cannot deal with them effectively. For example, you will probably arrive with some preconceived notions of your host culture. You will observe that all people do not share these "traits," and you will overlook them for some people while still believing them for the greater population. These two "truths" will need to live side by side in your mind, and you will learn to accept them and many others we explore further on in this chapter. Accept that, at the very least, you will at times feel confused and, at the extreme, close to certifiable! The self-contradictory nature of the paradox can do this to you. But if you let it, it can also strengthen your mind. [Note: dealing with paradox is one of *the* most critical skills those in the C-suite (offices of the chief executive, chief financial, chief operating officers and so on) must have, so learning to master this is a great advantage.]

Fourth, cultural mistakes and misunderstandings are inevitable. Learn from your blunders so you don't make them again, and be just as understanding when others make mistakes, too. Don't be afraid to publicly laugh at yourself; laughter can be a great equalizer and ice-breaker.

Fifth, the style and manner with which women seek solutions often gives us an advantage over our male counterparts in cross-cultural situations. For example, leverage your ability to build teams into a strong and powerful network across borders. Use your excellent communication skills to listen effectively and enable you to resolve tricky business situations in unfamiliar territory. Make the most of every single day.

Finally, keep a positive attitude. Some days will be more difficult than others, and you will need additional fortification. Devise a system that keeps your tank full, as it were, whether it's a daily workout routine, meditation in the morning, fresh flowers, the promise of regular travel, or contact with friends or family. Take care of yourself to ensure an upbeat and optimistic approach to the overall experience.

Making It Real

Before I moved to Mexico from Chile, my boss advised me not to say "in Chile we did it this way," or "back home it's like this." I have really tried to stay true to this advice, and it has worked. This is a different country, a different reality, and a different culture. No one really cares how great the place you left was, and they certainly don't want you to constantly compare the two.

They want you to accept and feel passionately about your new home.

– Claudia, Burson-Marstellar

As an American, our stereotypical reputation precedes us. Understanding the cultural and local norms of behavior and how we modify ours accordingly is paramount to our success. You do not want to be "the ugly American" because you're too loud, too opinionated, too passionate – characteristics that the American business world admires and rewards. Passionate is fine if you are posted in Spain, but a problem in Belgium. Understanding the context and dialing down helps you make a good first impression and strengthens your credibility. There is plenty of time for them to know the real you once you have an established track record.

– Diane, DuPont

Great leaders can find ways to lead in multiple cultural environments and be highly effective in doing so.

– Jackie, Alcon

As an American woman, doing business in Japan was difficult at first. I was used to sitting at the head of the table and leading meetings – not keeping quiet and listening to my male junior colleagues handle the discussion. At first, it made me mad – as if speaking to me directly wasn't good enough – plus, I noticed there were never any other women in the room. In time, however, I came to accept that in order to succeed, the most important thing was to be respectful of their way of doing things. We won contracts and grew the business, and I had to accept things the way they were. Such acceptance happened regularly – not necessarily by choice!

– Stacie, coauthor and consultant

Believe in yourself. There are times when you'll feel like everything is stacked against you. But remember, as a pioneer, you're bound to get a few arrows in your back. But it's all worth it when you lock in that first big win!

– Anna, former BP executive

As the first woman manager of an FAA security international field office in Singapore, I quickly learned that I had to be able to make good decisions fast. Singapore is twelve hours ahead of

Washington, D.C., so during my work day I had limited access to my colleagues back home. If I ran into a problem, which I did most days, I looked in the mirror, gave myself great advice, and made the leap! There's a much smaller safety net when you are outside HQ, so by definition, you learn to make your own decisions and learn how to manage the consequences of your choice – two of the most important skills you can acquire.

– **Mary, FAA**

It's important to have a sense of humor about it all and not be offended or disturbed if people laugh at you. You have to let a lot roll off your back. You have to be able to throw your ego out the window sometimes and be willing to look stupid.

– **Patricia,** *New York Times*

Making the Most of Being a Woman

As a woman you will be the recipient of a double dose of stereotyping: one for your nationality and the other for being a woman. The only thing you can do is to familiarize yourself with the generalizations and do your best to slowly but surely build relationships with people so they get to know you as an individual. Most women report that they are frequently told "you're not like a typical American woman," or "you don't act French" (or Japanese, or Australian or whatever). We find this fascinating because it sheds light on both the power of stereotyping and that of personal impressions. It's also one of the many paradoxes you'll encounter.

Whether you are traveling within your new country, regionally, or elsewhere around the world, you will be treated differently as a woman in each culture. Accept it, understand it, and modify your behavior accordingly. Don't frown upon the culture or try to change it – if you feel the need work with it to be successful. You will be respected for your efforts. Many women find the right balance and often can actually make more progress than if they were men. Often only a few women have gone before you, so you have a relatively clean slate on which to sketch your story. Here are a few lessons we've learned over the years.

Business Tips for Women

The business world remains predominantly a man's world. There are a few things you can do to prepare. First, **do not be offended if you are**

met with surprise or skepticism by male business counterparts. You might encounter a man who is surprised at your business role or position, and he might say something to that effect. Either ignore the comment or make light of it in a way that positions you as someone who understands he may not be used to dealing with women. Do not overreact. Do not say or do anything offensive until you better understand the cultural innuendos.

Second, **don't take offense if you continue to be treated differently from men.** Sometimes it can be nice to be treated differently; the upside of not having to compete in a vodka-shot competition or handshaking death grip in Russia is a real plus. But to feel completely ignored in a meeting in Korea can seem quite offensive. Don't be offended, but do not "get the coffee," "make the copies," or "leave a meeting" just because you are a woman. Act like a business professional, and eventually your new colleagues will accept you as one.

Third, **use your femaleness to your advantage, but do not do anything that jeopardizes your being taken seriously as a business professional.** You can, as many of us have done, flirt modestly, especially if it helps break the ice and enables you to work a little more easily with men. In some cultures, a little flirting is accepted as part of doing business; in others, however, it is frowned on and may be detrimental. Know the culture before you engage in this way. In the United States, political correctness and a litigious society have starched the human factor out of everyone. But in international markets throughout Europe and Latin America, a woman can more easily use her charm to her advantage.

Fourth, **observe the accepted protocol, and follow suit**. Greetings, business card exchanges, and language preference are examples of some of the differences. Watch others, and follow suit. For example, it may be customary for men to open doors, kiss women's hands as a greeting, or bow instead of shaking your hand. If it's not the custom to shake hands, do not insist; if you are asked to sit across from your business partner as opposed to next to him, do so. Try not to show offense even if you take it; some customs cannot be changed because they are part of the culture. What you believe is respect for you as a woman should come second to the respect owed you as a business professional. Equal respect and opportunity do not necessarily look the same in every culture.

If something angers you, such as the way men treat women in their own culture, stop and think before you charge others with insensitivity or male-chauvinist tendencies. Think about a particular aspect of your own culture, and try to put yourself in a foreigner's shoes when he or she experiences it. Try to understand a woman's role in local society. If, after many months of immersion in the local culture and strong efforts to understand it, you still feel extremely strongly about some particular issue in the local treatment of women, you may over time find ways to become a quietly effective advocate for change. But tread very carefully in this delicate space, keeping in mind how you would feel if someone from another culture were to get involved in controversial topics in your home country. If you decide that becoming an advocate for change is the right thing to do, you should confirm that (a) you feel very sure of your ground and are working with respected local women who agree with you, (b) you are prepared to spend some real time understanding and communicating effectively around the issue, and (c) both you and your employer are prepared to deal with any personal or professional consequences that might arise from your advocacy.

Making It Real

Today, many countries appear to have achieved equality of the sexes. But appearances can be deceiving, as most of the world's business community is still male-dominated. As a woman, it will be harder to be perceived as a leader. But with intelligence, persistence, cultural sensitivity, and feminine charm, you can do it!
— **Barbara, strategy and innovation Consultant**

Many of the Latin politicians with whom I engaged early on in my career simply didn't take me seriously. I think a lot of them couldn't believe I was a political officer looking for insights and information just like my male colleagues, so they often shared information with me that I'm convinced they would not have given to my male counterparts.
— **Donna, former U.S. Ambassador to Brazil, Venezuela, Bolivia, and the Dominican Republic**

When I started my career in Canada, I found it was a disadvantage to be a woman in a predominantly male profession of video postproduction. When I worked as an editor, clients would walk into the edit suite and some would walk out, refusing to work with a woman. But when I moved to Hong Kong, it didn't matter that I was a woman. I was a "gweilo" (foreign devil) with knowledge that they needed. I got four job offers on my first day of looking.

– Monique, The White Tulip

Age, experience, and presence count more than your sex.

– Mary, retired international director

In the 1990s, I worked on an assignment in Tunisia. To successfully complete our project, we needed information and input from a Tunisian government agency. My team leader (a man with decades of experience) had a great deal of difficulty securing that cooperation and was ultimately unable to get the agency to provide the information we needed. Finally, I agreed to go to the agency and see what I could find out. I very quickly obtained a meeting with a senior official who not only answered all my questions but gave me copies of important documents. I was astonished at my success! I subsequently found out from a Tunisian colleague that it is very rude in that society for men to say "no" to a woman. All I had to do was ask questions in a way that would make it uncomfortable for government officials (invariably men) to say "no" to me. I became the team's "point man" in gathering information from local sources, which ensured the success of our project. Sometimes it's all about being in the right place at the time and working it.

– Deborah, formerly PriceWaterhouse

I was often told that I didn't dress like a typical American woman. They told me I was much more feminine than people in Eastern Europe expected American women to be.

– Ruth, an international government agency

I learned early on to stand my ground. I may have been young and inexperienced compared with most people I was working and interacting with, but I relied on good judgment, honesty, and not backing down. I remember when I started working in Ekaterinburg, Russia, I was at a dinner with the heads of the local industrial enterprises – all men, of course. One man (I suppose it had been decided ahead of time) stood up and said in front of everyone sitting at the dinner table, "Why don't you just give us the project money and go home?" I stood up and said, "I am not going to turn over the money, and I am not going home, and we are going to stay and work on this project together, and I suggest we all have a toast to that." I then proceeded to raise my glass of vodka and gulp it down in one swoop.

– Karin, The Nature Conservancy

I accompanied my client to several universities in Indonesia to interview more candidates for a young professionals program. My job was to assess their English-language skills and then help the client determine the top fifty. We created a very objective measuring system, one that gave each candidate a quantitative score. When I presented the client with the results, they responded, "we can't take these candidates because they are women, they're religious conservatives, and they wear the full chadra." Their response blew my mind. It made me appreciate what tremendous opportunities I have – and take for granted – as an American woman.

– Laura, IBM Consulting

Accepting the Paradoxes of Life as an Expat

Paradoxes are a way of life in cross-cultural situations. Dealing with them day after day, week after week, is one of the best exercises you can do to expand and strengthen your mind. Recognize paradoxes when you see them, deal with them as best you can, and know that "no, you aren't going crazy;" it's just part of your life as a global citizen.

For her book *The Adventure of Working Abroad*, Dr. Joyce Sauters Osland, a professor of Social Organization at the University of Portland in Oregon, conducted research on the various kinds of paradoxes inherent in the business expatriate's life. She categorized them into four groups: relationships, perceptions, mediation, and identity. We agree with her premise and have expanded and contextualized her list for inclusion here:

1. Feeling powerful, yet playing down that power when necessary to be effective
2. Accepting cultural stereotypes, yet overlooking them for specific individuals you come to know

142

3. Growing to love a country but knowing there are things about it that don't suit your taste
4. Feeling at ease anywhere but as if you belong nowhere
5. Feeling caught between the demands of HQ and local realities
6. Representing the values of your company but realizing those values don't always coincide with the country you're in
7. Feeling free from your own cultural rules, yet realizing that many of those rules help you succeed
8. Suppressing some of your own cultural behaviors while finding other core cultural or national values strengthened
9. Becoming more worldly as a result of greater exposure, yet becoming more selective about which attributes you accept from various cultures
10. Feeling happy to see visitors from your own country, but feeling resentful when they act too "stereotypical."

Understand the Importance of Ethics in Business Around the World

Most companies maintain their own ethics and compliance rules, known as business ethics, which is a form of applied ethics. The aim of business ethics is to create a uniform sense within a company's employee population of how to conduct business responsibly. However, the term "ethics" can pose problems in an international context because the term does not translate well, and it can be difficult to find a common understanding of the term. Therefore, some organizations choose to recast the concept of business ethics through other terms, such as compliance, integrity, or responsible business practices. The field is vast, encompassing such concerns as corporate governance, accurate accounting and audits, and fair labor practices, just to name a few. Moreover, the field addresses the entire scope of a company's responsibilities to each of its stakeholders in its decisions and actions, such as employees, shareholders, suppliers, customers, and the community.

Make sure you understand your company's policies and follow them. Sometimes locally accepted business practices will conflict with your company's policies and code of ethics. Do not waver from your company's policy. Do not condone the local practices even if it means a competitive disadvantage. Resist the temptation to look the other way or bend the rules. Doing the right thing will bring its own rewards in the long run. You may even find that your company can help improve local practice. Below we highlight a few important principles to keep in mind as you do business in an overseas market.

1. **Make sure you understand both the local laws and your company's policies on potentially troublesome business practices, especially the "gray" areas.** Many times a perfectly legal and acceptable local manner of doing business is not allowed by one's company headquartered abroad. For example, small bribes, gifts, and entertainment are acceptable in some countries, yet strictly prohibited or proscribed by some company policies.

2. **Familiarize yourself with the most common practices you are likely to encounter**, such as competition and antitrust laws; facilitating payments as covered by USA, EU, and international laws; foreign corrupt practices act; money laundering regulations; diversity issues, work place discrimination and sexual harassment regulations, and intellectual property rights.

3. **Be aware that some employment practices may seem unethical according to your cultural norms but aren't in the country you're working in.** You need to check your company's policy against the accepted local laws and operate in a way consistent with its policies. For example, outside the United States, gender, age, or religion may be adequate and accepted reasons not to hire someone – but probably not if your company is an American one.

4. **Err on the side of being conservative.** Be prepared to make judgment calls when no one is around to help and the situation is awkward. The risks and penalties of getting on the wrong side of a legal or ethics issue are too high.

Making It Real

While staying at the hotel, I purchased some gifts for the family at the gift shop, which were charged directly to my room. Upon checkout I insisted that the hotel clerk separate those charges from the business expenses to which my joint venture partner said, "It's not much money…go ahead and put it on the company bill." It was an opportunity to set the right tone. I told him that it was important that we keep personal and business expenses separate as a matter of principle and that failure to do so would not only jeopardize the success of the joint venture but compromise our business ethics.

– Anna, former BP executive

Never be afraid to ask questions or seek advice on matters that seem to cross the line in any aspect of your business dealings. As most HR professionals will attest, there's no such thing as a dumb question from someone living in another country and culture. There's a great deal to learn, cope with, and enjoy during your first year overseas. Whether they are learning the ropes of being a new woman on the block, encountering the slippery slopes of sticky ethical situations, or dealing with the mind-bending paradoxes of being a global citizen, our globetrotting women have been there, and three will share their tales from the front.

The Journey Continues

Anna

Setting the right tone proved critical throughout my time in China as I set about establishing a downstream (refining/marketing) business for Amoco to serve as a beachhead for eventually moving into the lucrative retail market. At the time, China was developing its energy infrastructure – transportation, home heating, industrial, etc. – and the opportunities were numerous. It was a matter of finding the right business – which turned out to be LPG (liquefied petroleum gas) and the right partner.

Upon investigation we found an interesting partner in Huaneng Energy Company, the largest electrical company in China. The company had strong government connections and was being advised by a former Chinese oil industry executive. Preliminary discussions seemed to indicate that they too had strong interest in meeting with us, and so I prepared to go into formal negotiations for the deal. Now it's important to understand that I had never negotiated anything more substantial than a salary increase (and I don't think I was very successful at that!), so I put out a call for backup! Interestingly, the two people who came to my rescue were both women: Amoco's controller and one of the lead corporate commercial attorneys. They flew over to Beijing and spent May Day weekend in my conference room helping me hash through the salient commercial issues and our negotiation strategy.

The following week we walked into the negotiation room – picture this: our team led by three women representing Amoco, sitting across the table from a team of Chinese men! They must have been both stunned and amused; I'm sure it had never happened before. I quickly saw that negotiations from the other side of the table were being led by a Mr. Zhong, a diminutive man who looked as if he was in his late 60s or early 70s. We exchanged the normal pleasantries, and the potential partners learned that I was Chinese American, that my father was from Ningbo (close to the site of the proposed JV,) and that I spoke Mandarin. We dived into a morning of negotiations (via translation for the benefit of our whole team). During a break, after about five hours of negotiating, Mr. Zhong called me to the side and told me that the Huaneng team liked us, and they felt we would be good partners. Moreover, he told me that my "competition" were all Japanese companies, and even though he knew the Japanese companies would likely be involved in supplying the deal, they were from the Nanjing area (a town that suffered greatly under the hands of the Japanese in 1937), so he preferred to have an American company as the primary partner. He said, "Let's make this work." Sure enough, by the end of the day we had a deal.

As I look back on my career, pulling the JV together was one of the most challenging projects I was ever involved in – and one of my proudest accomplishments. From the first meeting throughout the months of discussion before the groundbreaking, there were many milestones in the joint venture journey. Topics of suppliers, contractors, construction safety, employees, and commercial strategy tested our values and policies and forced decisions on how we would work together. Today, because of the BP/Amoco merger and the subsequent purchase of ARCO, the joint venture is the largest LPG business in China. Much progress has come from that fateful day when three women ventured to the negotiation table filled with men!

Perry

The first hundred days in a new position is always difficult. But to my surprise, it proved even more so when I moved to a new market in a role that was created more to fulfill my desire to live in London than to meet an immediate business need for the company. I was so excited to finally get there I didn't care that I didn't have a "big job" upon arrival. At least I was a managing director and the head of HR for the European corporate practice. The company agreed to put me in London because that was where I wanted to be. My bosses from both Singapore and Russia days were now based in Western Europe, and they vouched for me. The "collective thinking" was that since I'd succeeded in two previous regions for the firm, I would find a way to do so again. It was a risk, as I'd never worked for this firm in a sophisticated communications market like London, but they were willing to try because of my track record.

I immediately threw myself into the challenges before me. Having no formal background in HR but a lot of experience managing different types of professionals enabled me to offer new perspectives. I had learned from real world experience that common sense, motivation, and emotional intelligence are often stronger indicators of success than family ties or advanced degrees. By applying this knowledge, I was able to contribute from day one. But I knew that, especially as an expat I would need to do much more for the agency to keep me in London for the longer term. And I wanted to stay.

Luckily for me, a few weeks after I arrived, a request came in from one of the firm's largest global clients, Unilever. They wanted some help in – of all places – Russia. My boss suggested that the existing client team take me to the meeting, as it was nearby and I had a lot of Russian know-how. (This proved a fateful decision as that meeting set up my opportunity to succeed in London as well as my opportunity for a great move back to the United States more than three years later.) Despite being a female and an American (two potential strikes against me in the European old-boys network), I was able to help the team win the business, thanks to my Russia credentials and common-sense approach to assessing the company's needs in that market. Two weeks later, the win put me back at Sheremetyevo airport, only this time I brought just a carry-on bag and my laptop. Within a few months, the success of the work we did in Russia led to new assignments across all of Unilever Central and Eastern Europe. Then, as often happens, one regional president talked with another, and soon I was also supporting Unilever businesses in Latin America.

Less than four months after moving to London, I had set up home in a lovely little mews house near Hyde Park, made some great new friends, found a wonderful man, and created a role important enough to secure my position in London. Within the year, we grew that client into the firm's largest worldwide – thus proving the "collective thinking" to be right and teaching me that I could find a way to add value in almost any new opportunity if I was willing to use what I knew, learn what I didn't know, and pursue an opportunity aggressively. Of course, having a bit of luck didn't hurt either.

Diane

Doing business in numerous markets requires adaptability and flexibility. However, the one instance in which "adaptability" is not warranted, in my opinion, is ethics. You must know your corporate culture to do the right thing, regardless of whether or not you get any ethics training. Some companies are less strict than others, but DuPont prides itself on maintaining the highest level of business ethics in every country in which we operate around the world. This constant actually helped me through many situations in which the ground rules were a bit murky. For example, I have found that Europeans are far more willing to meet and talk with competitors than Americans are. I often found myself in conversations that wandered close to the edge of what is appropriate to discuss. I had the courage to speak up – I had to, for the topic was too close to the edge for me to be comfortable. I didn't care if I sounded like an over-legalized American or was perceived as coming across as "holier than thou." After many uncomfortable situations, it has become my policy – and I recommend the same to others – to invite my local lawyer to join me in meetings with competitors – this practice helps me make sure I stay out of trouble. Sometimes my competitors have resisted the lawyer's inclusion. . . then I absolutely bring my lawyer with me! No deal is worth doing if it costs you your job.

148

Chapter 7

Year Two and Beyond: Distinguishing Yourself

The hardest part of building an international career is typically getting that first overseas job. Once you've gotten it, however, you still have to make the most of it. I parlayed success in Singapore into a bigger and better role in Moscow and then did it again to get my dream job in London. With planning and effort, you can literally work your way around the world.

— Perry, coauthor and Kraft Foods, Inc.

Once you've gotten a good handle on your job and have proved you can deliver, it's time to start figuring out how to distinguish yourself. You have talent. You work hard. You've cleared the hurdles of working overseas, and now it's time to make a name for yourself – to shine brighter than the other talented, hard-working colleagues around you and back in your home office or HQ. To do that you generally need to aspire to greater and more expansive roles. Take on new challenges and responsibilities, especially general management and line roles that may be more difficult to land back home, and then market your successes. If you do so successfully, you will continue to fast-track your career and provide more personal options as you move ahead professionally.

While expanding your role, *never* let the job you were hired to do suffer. Fulfilling your current responsibilities while taking on more challenging roles can prove to be extremely difficult. Do not take on more than you can handle, but recognize that hard work is part of the game. One of the realities of working abroad is the long hours: these jobs are definitely *not* 9 to 5. Consider one year in which you will work, on average, fourteen-hour days and half the weekends to be equal to an extra year of career experience. Make sure not only that you think like this (for it will help you keep your sanity when you're wondering why you're working so hard) but that you tell colleagues, mentors, and HR the same. People who have not worked outside their home turf do not always understand the tremendous growth that takes place in those who work abroad.

If after one year you are still finding your way, figure out why. Be honest with yourself. Is it the position and your skills? Is it your team or your supervisor? Are you having difficulty coping with the foreign environment? Is the expectancy either unreasonable or have you not made some critical adjustment? Is your personal situation adversely affecting your ability to do your job well? Whatever the reason, you need to do something about it. Sometimes people have to return early, take a break, or get help from HR or outside advisers. It's ok to ask for help, and it may be necessary to your personal well-being and professional standing. You may also find that the assistance gets you over your hurdle so that you can continue overseas. Or you may find it's a lifeline to rescue and you return back home. As we noted earlier, overseas positions are not right for everyone. Do what's right for you, for after all, the international assignment is meant to propel you forward, not set you back.

Expanding Your Profile

The average international assignment is for three years. As we saw in Chapter 6, getting the job done well is the top priority, and it will probably take you about a year to get used to your new position, colleagues, and environment. Our advice in this chapter is based on the second stage, beginning about a year or so into your assignment. If you've begun to operate successfully, than you're ready to start branching out. Think strategically about your next steps. You might consider taking on additional assignments, solving some of the tricky problems you might have encountered early on but didn't know how to address, or building relationships beyond your current circle to expand your options. Such actions are parallel to those you may have considered or undertaken when landing your international posting.

Identifying Business Needs

Although some people know exactly how they plan to get ahead, most of us don't. Some of us just keep our eyes open and make the most of every situation we encounter. Sometimes luck is involved: life throws us into a business situation that demands solutions we are able to find.

The most important thing you can do – whether you have a plan or not – is to pay thoughtful attention to what is going on. Monitor business trends, pay attention to national events as well as global events that may affect your market, and use your contacts with local clients, customers, and business organizations to keep your finger on the pulse of what could be coming up next. Examine critical business issues at hand, and make a list of the three most pressing ones you believe you have a solution for. Take the easiest one first – easiest in the sense that success is most likely and can be effected most quickly. It doesn't have to be huge or earth-shattering; it just needs to be beyond your daily job. Do it, but be careful not to step on someone else's toes. Exercise good political judgment, and don't take over someone else's territory when you take on assignments to expand your role.

When your company is looking for people to take on additional projects, raise your hand, especially if they're the projects that others don't want to take. You'll earn points for helping out, and you'll inevitably get to meet more people, solve more problems, and credit more wins to your name. If the project bombs or doesn't turn out as well as you'd like, accept your responsibility, learn the relevant lessons, and move on. Connect with your supervisor to ensure you both understand what happened and how to avoid similar problems in the future.

Making It Real

Once I got a handle on how to manage the plant, I was able to morph the standard plant supervisor job into one that I could add real value to by using my customer and sales skills. It had been a while since a customer visited the plant, so we worked as a team to create a series of customer site visits. In the two years I was there, more than a hundred customers toured our facility. We solicited their feedback and used this insight to enhance our productivity. Our customer satisfaction improved significantly, and our cost productivity was excellent. HQ noticed our great results.

– Diane, DuPont

Although I have advanced throughout my career, my track has been more about self-actualization as opposed to vertical advancement. China has helped me achieve this in leaps and bounds.

– Angie, Hudson Recruitment

Arriving in Russia on Christmas Eve was no picnic. However, I saw the opportunity for line management responsibility at an early stage in my career, and I took it. The chance to practice the lost art of general management – running all aspects of an operation, from product development to staffing to facilities to payroll – is tough to get these days in large American companies unless you're already a senior manager. The problem is, having general management experience is also what most of the top jobs are all about, so it's critical to have if you want to reach the C-suite!

– Perry, coauthor and Kraft Foods, Inc.

Networking Locally

Build relationships with local colleagues. Experiencing local life with your colleagues usually adds a dimension you would miss if you only worked with them. Show your willingness to accept their hospitality and enjoy their company, and offer yours in return. Don't confuse – or let others confuse – your spending time with your team as anything other than good business practice.

These better relationships will result in a more effective means to manage the dynamic tension between local and HQ demands. This toggling between two points of view will most likely prove to be one of the most challenging aspects of your time overseas. If you have been sent to the field by HQ, you'll be expected to see things from their perspective. This is difficult because your local "mind" and team will incline you toward making a local decision. It takes courage and diplomacy to inform HQ when their recommendation is not the best solution. It will also require the same when you tell your local teammates that the HQ decision is best overall. Don't lose sight of both the local and global roles for which you are responsible. Successfully managing both perspectives will make you a better manager – no doubt about it.

Finally, join a professional organization. Doing so will enable you to meet more people, better appreciate the local business situation within the greater context of broader perspectives, improve your credibility, and discover opportunities to expand your role. Research the one or two that will best help you meet your objectives, and join, don't overextend yourself by joining too many. Get to know the players and network, network, network!

Making It Real

After doing business in China for seven years, I took on role of chairman of the U.S. Chamber of Commerce for China. In that capacity, I served as spokesperson for more than two thousand businesses on a variety of topics involving U.S. interests in China. I had the opportunity to meet with and discuss potential solutions with members of the Chinese Government, former U.S. Presidents, CEOs of Fortune 500 companies, and other leading members of the political and business communities who want their voice to be heard in China. It would have taken me three to four times as long to achieve the same status – if ever – back in the States.

– Angie, Hudson Recruitment

I have found that the strongest business relationships result from spending some entertainment or personal time with the various people involved. You can cement relationships not only with your counterparts but also with colleagues from your own company with whom you travel and share experiences over time. This enables you to work better as a team and learn how to leverage each other's respective skill sets. In addition, the friendships you will undoubtedly form will last a lifetime.

– Jackie, Alcon

As you work across cultures, you will encounter people who approach situations from a different perspective. Use this new ground to learn how to effectively step into their shoes, whether it's a customer, an employee, or even those back in HQ. Learn how to work through the differences by understanding the other perspective(s), not only so that you're successful in that particular situation, but so that this new way of doing business becomes part of your ongoing style.

— **Diane, DuPont**

Building Relationships With HQ

Employees who have relocated are usually high on senior management's radar screen. You are positioned for greater access to senior leaders of your company; use it to your advantage. Most of the professional women we interviewed were either put on regional internal management boards, showcased at global leadership meetings, or asked to serve on challenging project teams — often high-risk, high-profile ones — because of their accomplishments in markets outside their home turf. Keep your eyes open for such opportunities. You may even suggest such ideas through HR, your former supervisor, or your mentor.

Take advantage of your position to invite members of the C-suite to your locale for a client meeting, for a business conference, or simply as a way of showing support for the location — and you. When they accept, offer to serve as their local host to ensure you'll get plenty of face time with them. By doing so, you'll see a completely different side of them as they operate outside their own market. The success of your own adaptation will no doubt impress them. This can work especially well if you're middle management: sophisticated enough to carry on a conversation with a senior leader of a global company, but not senior enough to report directly to them, which sets up a hierarchical dynamic.

Make the most of your home visits by planning a stopover in HQ to network with senior management and former colleagues. It is imperative that you maintain your profile in the HQ country. Set up meetings with senior leaders, including those who visited you, to give them a snapshot of how you're doing, share your successes, and, if necessary, request specific advice. Be sure to be brief — no more than thirty minutes — and leave them with the impression that you know what you are doing, and you're doing it well. In addition, arrange meetings with those who can help you manage your career, such as HR, a specific business leader, and your mentor. It's also important to touch base with old colleagues and friends — the people you used to work with and may again upon your return.

Making It Real

One of the most important things I learned while working abroad is that I can achieve most anything if I build the right relationships.

– Joanne, USAID

Relationships with senior leaders are critical to ongoing success. Mine opened many doors for me because I was able to arrange meetings between them and existing and potential clients in Hong Kong. My stature increased, and my consulting relationships grew quickly with these clients because they valued my ability to deliver our CEO when they needed senior business advice.

– Stacie, coauthor and consultant

Finding a Mentor

Experience indicates that the best mentor for the international professional is either a former expat or a senior leader with global responsibility. This person will help you ride the waves as you complete your initial assignment and choose to move on or return. He or she will also play a critical role by representing you during your absence, so the more senior the person the better. You might wonder: why would the COO want to mentor little ol' you? It's because these leaders recognize that "not just anyone will do" in mentoring a professional who is currently overseas. Emphasize the importance of a senior global leader playing a role in your career development.

Marketing Your Success

In Chapter 2, we advised you how best to market yourself so as to land a global assignment. Do it again – this time to parlay your international experience into your next big role. Demonstrate that you are the kind of person who makes things happen. Consider how best you can package your successes to systematically showcase them to the right people and make the most of impromptu encounters. As you do both, it's critical that the content of your achievements be made relevant to the target audiences. No one wants to just listen to you going on about your great achievements; there must be something in it for *them* – for their business unit, their team, their position. However, the most important step to take – especially if you are planning on returning to HQ – is to find the most effective way to communicate with senior leaders there. Remember, the overall objective is to showcase how you have accomplished great things for the company in unfamiliar territory.

Making It Real

There's a big "wow" factor expressed by senior leaders when you spend time with them abroad that cannot be underestimated. Senior leadership paid attention to me. Whenever one of them had a trip to the region, he would take the time to meet with me, take me to dinner, and simply get a feel for how I was doing and what was going on. Many of them also made time to see me on every trip I made back to New York. This high-level attention and interaction helped my career in two ways: those at the top got to know me better, and it made me a more loyal and dedicated employee because I knew they cared.

– Stacie, coauthor and consultant

During my three years in Belgium, I went back to HQ often to keep up my contacts. I knew I wanted to return after my three-year stint and recognized how important my network was while I was away. This network helped me when I began lobbying for my return (about one year in advance). I returned to a great job and now strive to maintain the network I built in Europe!

– Rebecca, ExxonMobil

Listed below are some tips on how to ensure the basics are covered in making the most of your successes.

1. Be sure that **your work is adequately documented** in your performance reviews. Request that you have a review every six months so that you and your supervisor can keep track of your achievements. Share these reviews with your global HR representative.

2. **Identify the people** who want to know, who should know, and who can help you move ahead – in the country, in the region, and eventually back home. You never know when you might have the opportunity to meet with members of your growing network.

3. **Package your successes** so that they quantify and qualify your accomplishments: those that were part of your original job description

156

and those you took on as your own initiative.

4. **Enlist allies** to help you tell your story. Although you should be able to tell it yourself eloquently enough, there is much more credibility when someone else does it for you.

If you do your job well and assume additional responsibilities, you will have an awesome experience to share – and to leverage into your next position.

Your Assignment is Coming to an End

Twelve months or so before your contract is due to end, you should begin negotiating your next step with your company: first, to allow yourself plenty of time to consider, and second, because the process tends to take longer than you otherwise might think. You have some choices to make. What's best for you? Where do you want to go next? What do you want to do? How you position your experience will matter a great deal. All options require careful consideration and a great deal of time and attention. You and your company may agree that staying on for another year or two is best. You may be offered a position in another market. You may be at odds with your company's recommendation on what to do next. You may decide to return home; if so, Chapter 8 provides the details on how to ensure a successful return. If, however, you're not ready to go back, consider these options:

- **Expand your current role in the same market**. If you'd like to stay, you'll need to determine if your current position and financial remuneration are satisfactory. If you are consistently performing above your current level, negotiate for a better title, salary, and overall package. Keep in mind that your organization may opt to offer you a local package, which you will need to examine to ensure that you are actually moving forward, given that currency fluctuations, housing prices, and local taxes, for example, may eat up a substantial portion of your income. Most experts agree that five to six years makes you a "local expert," while more than ten years generally means you are more local than global. Many professionals, including HR experts, believe expatriates are less likely to be able to integrate back into their home country after more than ten years abroad. For the women who went local, most say it was one of the best decisions they ever made because it gave them the freedom to make their own choices as opposed to satisfying company needs. Make sure you understand the benefits and the risks.

- **Change companies but stay in the same market**. You may decide that you want to stay, but your company wants you to return. Or you may have found another organization that you prefer. Whatever the reason, make sure you completely understand all the fine print in switching employers, and don't just assume you're your prospective employer has all the facts. Many governments have rules restricting changes, and you wouldn't want to be suspended helplessly in a tangled web of bureaucracy.

- **Move to another location with the same company**. The more countries you have direct experience living and working in, the more global you become. Plus, the relative ease with which a company can move an international employee from one country to the next, coupled with your proven ability to adapt and deliver in a foreign environment, creates a level of comfort and confidence for both parties. You are simply a lower risk. If you are willing to move to a new market, reread the material in Chapters 3 and 4 about markets and negotiating the deal. You will revisit many of the same preparatory considerations you did before your original move, but this time you'll be much wiser. You will probably have more ability to choose your next destination because you've become a known quantity in the global workforce. Use your increased profile to your advantage as you begin to shop around. Most of the women who took this route did so for two main reasons: they wanted additional geographic exposure, and they took a job that added a skill, level, or position to their portfolio that they felt they couldn't acquire as easily in their home market, such as line manager for a company's country operation or local manufacturing plant.

- **Switch companies and move to another market**. For reasons similar to changing companies locally, you may decide to switch companies and countries. Some women who switched did so upon their return to their home markets; some outgrew their former companies, and some wanted to return, but the company couldn't find the right role for them. Follow the advice above for both, and make sure you pay attention to the fine print.

Making It Real

While most successful professionals are promoted to the next level every three to five years, it's been rare for me to be in the same job for twenty-four months. I've moved within the same firm and, when necessary, between firms. Several of the moves I made were ones I sought. Some were more company initiated. Every region and every role was a new challenge and a new adventure. Looking back, I wouldn't have wanted to miss a single destination. In the process, it was hard work. What I learned was that securing your next job requires both that you do your current job extremely well and that you actively position yourself for the role you want next – at the same time. By aligning my goals with those of my firm, being open to different opportunities, and taking some big risks, I was always able to land that next great job. You can too!

– Perry, coauthor and Kraft Foods, Inc.

Although the senior leaders back in Wilmington encouraged me to return to the United States after two and a half years in Switzerland, I wasn't ready to go back. I wanted to stay in Europe. I felt I needed additional overseas experience to build out my skillset. My requests were supported, and I was offered a plant supervisor role in Belgium.

– Diane, DuPont

I ran into all kinds of local bureaucratic snags when I became a local Nestlé hire and then even more when I switched to a different employer, Swissair. Although many aspects of the change were extremely difficult, my experience in the Swissair bankruptcy was priceless in terms of what I learned about running a business.

– Jackie, Alcon

There is much to be learned, gained, and leveraged while you are working abroad. Remember that perceptions of you will naturally evolve. After about two years of living and working overseas, you will be recognized as "international" or "global." You will have earned your stripes and

159

the credibility that comes with that, since you have been on the other side and lived and worked on the ground.

The Journey Continues

Jackie

While working on the Alcon business for Nestlé at their headquarters for three years, I broadened my skill set, increased my confidence, and enjoyed the European lifestyle. Since I was not quite ready to return home to Texas after my term ended, I began to explore my options within Nestlé. As a result of having built up my network by delivering a solid track record of performance and demonstrating a constant willingness to take on any and every project (especially the ones no one else wanted to touch!), my reputation grew. Although it was risky to jump from a familiar smaller company to one of the world's largest, and to do so as a local hire, I did it believing the potential for a big pay-off justified those risks.

Critical to my continued success was finding the right position. To do so, I solicited advice from senior leaders within the organization. Some of them I knew, and some I didn't; but I figured I'd give it a shot and would ask for a thirty-minute meeting with those in a position to know how best to help me achieve my goals. It usually worked. People were happy to advise me, especially if I adequately articulated what I was hoping to accomplish for myself and the company, and why. After considering their combined advice, I accepted a job as Deputy Treasurer, the job with the potential for broadest experience and most exposure.

For the next two years, I worked with colleagues in countries all over the world, working with all kinds of business units and affiliates to create a centralized finance system that had not previously existed within a company as global and decentralized as Nestlé. This was tough, as I had to sell the idea to business leaders in more than a hundred countries that centralizing was actually better for them. I brought a combination of technical solutions and an ability to sell ideas well and manage the process to their satisfaction. The net result was a more sophisticated, centralized finance system that created a more consistent global philosophy for managing financial positions and risk, which reflected itself in improved income statement results and more predictability of borrowing costs, investment

160

earnings, and currency impacts. After two years, and at the age of only thirty-seven, I was named Nestlé's Treasurer. I reported to the CFO.

Soon after I took on this role, the financial markets around the world began to have serious problems. During the next three years, I managed multiple crises for Nestlé and its affiliates as the Asian markets, Russia, Brazil, and then Turkey took turns crashing, toppling local economies and flattening budding markets in some instances. I learned that I had the right combination of decisiveness, guts, and presence of mind to handle the stress as we emerged, one market at a time, from these financial disasters. Although I wouldn't say that I thrived on these tumultuous times, I grew exponentially learning in leaps and bounds about myself and the global marketplace. This role prepared me for my next one: CFO of Swissair, a $17 billion global company with 70,000 employees.

One day I got a call from my former boss and mentor, who was the new CEO of Swissair Group. He offered me the position of CFO. Although it was risky – the airline had been reported to be having financial difficulties, I would be working in an unfamiliar industry, and I would be switching companies as a local hire – I went for it. Within three months, right after 9/11, Swissair filed for bankruptcy. I felt that all of the preparation, planning, and learning thus far would be used as I worked through the bankruptcy process.

Diane

My pan-European role challenged me in its complexity as I dealt with multiple countries, cultures, languages, and even currencies before the Euro was introduced. Italians, French, Swiss, and Brits were reporting to me, while I reported to a Brit. The intricacies of cross-European professional politics had to be learned, and there was so much newness to the management side that I felt fortunate that the essential nature of my role – customers and sales – stayed the same. I dove in. As I look back, I believe a great deal of my success, then and now, stems from my patience and tolerance of difference. I knew what it was like to be in the minority and endure stereotypes.

I needed this high level of awareness and understanding when I became the first American woman to supervise a European plant – a role

161

that was important to me because I needed the all-important plant responsibility to keep moving up the DuPont corporate ladder. Plus, Belgium sounded like more fun than West Virginia! But I was going out on a limb. While the plant made products with which I was familiar, I hadn't had a role in a plant since the very beginning of my career. In addition, this one ran 24/7 in a country I didn't know very well and was on the site of a larger DuPont plant operation, run by a plant manager from Luxembourg, who did not see any value in my skills. In fact, he viewed me as a liability: an American who didn't speak the language, who hadn't run a plant, and who would probably fail on his turf. I was taking a huge risk in transitioning from my pan-European customer and sales role into a national plant role. For the first time in my life, I doubted my own ability. Determined to do my best, I created teams and learned to speak Dutch. I took a humble approach, exposed my vulnerabilities, and brainstormed with colleagues as to how I could add value. We came up with some terrific solutions and instituted tremendous change.

Throughout my entire time in Belgium, I relied on my strengths to carry me through, and I worked *hard*. I learned how to handle my boss by proactively meeting with him weekly. But he still wasn't interested in teaching me much. So I began to build relationships with other plant managers – senior manufacturing guys, across Europe who taught me a tremendous amount about manufacturing and how to make effective change. In fact, our team won the prestigious DuPont award, the Sustainable Growth Award, for our work in eliminating heavy metal from plastics. This elimination was cutting-edge in the 1990s and one of the accomplishments for which I am most proud. As a team, we couldn't have achieved it had we not first learned to work together, trust one another, and make progress toward our common goal.

These two different roles overseas made an enormous difference in my career. My skill set evolved and developed, and I learned so much I felt like a sponge soaking up knowledge from everyone and every project. When the opportunity came for me to return to the United States, I was ready. I knew I'd miss the overseas component, but I just couldn't turn down the offer to work directly with DuPont's CEO back in Wilmington.

Stacie

I went to Asia as a middle manager and returned to the United States three years later as a senior leader. During that time, I expanded my technical skills and operated as a senior leader, first in Hong Kong and then around the region. I joined the office as a member of the local leadership team and left as a member of a regional leadership team. I earned the respect of my local clients – many of them regional presidents – who came to value my global perspective coupled with local knowledge. The regional executive management team appreciated the cutting-edge skills I had acquired and honed in the United States, and they were patient with me as I learned the Asian ropes. I built a close relationship with the global board back in New York, with whom I made a name for myself. Not only did I bring fresh, forward-thinking PR solutions to local and multinational companies, but my interpersonal and listening skills inspired my team to great heights despite the rapidly declining local and regional economies in the late 1990s.

As a result of my increasingly high-profile position, I became a role model for and a mentor to future expat women. My relationships with the C-suite led not only to my smooth return to home base, but also enabled me to have business discussions and debates with the senior leaders of the firm. They were always there for me when I needed client advice or just a senior person on the line or in a meeting with one of my regional clients. My counseling skills and business acumen increased manifold as I regularly spent time with business leaders with twenty or more years of experience.

One of my clients was the agency's second largest, Accenture, first in Hong Kong and then regionally as I grew the business to seven-figures within only three years. I was the regional leader of the agency's second largest client and was a member of its global team. Unbeknownst to me at the time, I had the opportunity to work with my future boss, a Canadian working in New York who had lived in Hong Kong, Singapore, and The Netherlands. He became my mentor and is still a good friend today. While I was in Hong Kong and during those first few years back in the States, his global experience helped ease my transition. He empathized with me as I expressed my frustration, coached me on how best to use my global skills to propel me forward, and served as my advocate on the internal executive management team. He not only understood the global dimensions of the business, but also valued and appreciated them. If you can find such a friend or mentor when you move to another market and then eventually return home, he or she will be instrumental in your successful return.

Perry

In ten years living and working abroad, I was able to move up, from region to region, right around the world, mostly with the same employer. None of the moves was especially easy professionally or personally. But I was able to map out my own path by knowing what I wanted personally and what I needed professionally, and then going after it. Like most careers, mine developed in stages, role after role, each building upon the previous one. It was not exactly the path I had envisioned from my youth, but it was more exciting and more rewarding than I ever imagined possible.

Once I joined B-M in Singapore, I worked hard every day to earn my keep. Late nights and weekend work were the norm, with a bit of water skiing or windsurfing on the side. My commitment to my clients, most notably DuPont and Citibank, coupled with good counsel, solid execution, and lots of networking, made it easy for the firm to classify me as a keeper. Because I delivered, the company kept offering me different roles and then new markets whenever I was beginning to feel the need for a change of venue, which turned out to be about every three years. For example, about a year into running the firm's public education efforts to support Russian economic reform, I persuaded the company to let me open a commercial office to complement the privatization work. This gave me a whole new set of challenges. It also helped me negotiate my way onto the European Board – a move that ensured that while I was running a relatively small business, I would have regular face time with the head of the region as well as the rest of the European market leaders. I'm convinced this made a huge difference in securing my next posting.

I took several months off after Russia to recharge my batteries, spend time with family and friends in the United States, and think about what I really wanted to do next. I considered a lot of options during that time off, including giving up business altogether and going to grad school to study political science. Just as I was seriously beginning to plot out a career in politics, the company approached me with the idea of moving to Europe. I told them that if they would make it London, they had a deal. They said yes. (I'm sure the fact that I was still "relatively cheap" as expats go, being young and single, didn't hurt either.)

From move to move, I've always thought of career development like a set of building blocks. My early years in the United States and Asia provided a strong foundation and helped me master the principles and practices of my profession and the art of client management. The next level, Russia, added core infrastructure – general management experience and leadership development in a less-than-hospitable market environment, all while operating mainly in a second language. Then there was London, a "penthouse" opportunity that taught me about delivering world-class counsel to global clients and effectively managing colleagues around the world. All this learning came together and made a senior in-house move possible, first at Unilever and later at Kraft. While the range of my corporate affairs experience got me into the candidate pool, it was my international experience, encompassing both developing and developed markets, that truly set me apart.

Patricia

As a journalist I have a little different story. I witnessed many dramatic and historic moments in the former Soviet Union, especially in Moscow. When Gorbachev was on vacation at a Black Sea resort, some of the government's most hard-line members took him prisoner, intending to install one of their own as the new leader of the fifteen-republic Soviet Union. Immediately, the Soviet Army ordered Army tanks into the city of Moscow to take control of the so-called White House, the seat of the Russian government. To get there, the tanks had to drive down Kutuzovsky Prospekt, a broad avenue that was near both my apartment and the *BusinessWeek* bureau. I'll never forget the awesome sound of those tank treads grinding up the asphalt as they slowly made their way down the avenue. I ran the half mile or so to the entrance to the White House, where the first tank stopped. The whole line came to a halt, and everything was still. The soldiers stayed hidden in their tanks, apparently waiting for orders. My first thought was, come on, Russians, drive up the buses! Drive up the trucks! Block the gates before the tanks go in!

But on the other side of the White House, one Russian was taking charge. This was Boris Yeltsin, president of the republic of Russia. Knowing that he was next on the list to be arrested, and smelling a political opportunity, he climbed aboard one of the tanks and rallied the people to resist. The tanks didn't storm the White House, but neither did they retreat. The citizens of Moscow finally set up a blockade, and teenage boys guarded every door. As a journalist, I had a press pass to go inside. On the second evening, I was interviewing politicians and others who had gathered inside when the Mayor of Moscow Sergei Stankevich got on the PA system and said, "All women and children, please leave the building. We have been monitoring the security radio waves, and the KGB troops have been ordered to storm the White House. They're on their way!" Now, I wanted to witness history, but I didn't want to die doing it, especially for a business publication. I wanted to get out of there. I slowly made my way through the labyrinthine hallways. Once I got to the exit, the teen guards were so intent on protecting the building that they almost didn't let me out. I pushed my way through, and in a drizzling rain, I waited and waited. The troops never came. After three days, the right-wing coup leaders gave up and released Gorbachev. When Yeltsin strode out onto the balcony of the White House to celebrate and lead a huge rally of cheering Russians, I was standing just fifteen feet away from him. When *BusinessWeek* ran the picture of Yeltsin and the rally on the cover, I look like a white speck, but I know it's me!

The story we did the next week is the one that I am most proud of. Rose Brady, the *BusinessWeek* bureau chief, and I decided we wanted to do reporting in some of the other republics. In Kiev, the capital of Ukraine, I interviewed parliamentarians, people on the street, shopkeepers, and business people. Everyone said that Ukraine should break away from the Soviet Union and declare independence. I took the overnight train back, and found out from Rose that people in the Baltic republics were saying the same thing. We proposed doing a cover story that would say the Soviet

Union was about to disintegrate. This doesn't sound courageous or surprising in retrospect. But we proposed doing this story in mid-August 1991. The Soviet Union officially dissolved in December 1991. We had to lobby our editors in New York to convince them to run this as their cover story. No one else was reporting it at the time. They trusted us and ran the cover. I remember being scared, thinking, *gee, I'm just a stringer and we're running a major story based on my 12 hours in Kiev.* By the time the USSR collapsed, I was back home in Washington, D.C. Boy, was I proud and relieved when the events we predicted actually came to pass.

The combination of my hard work, my ability to spot a good story, and my close-knit network of influential people in Moscow all paid off. By the summer of 1996, the bureau chief went back to the United States and *BusinessWeek* made me Moscow bureau chief and a full-time staffer with all the benefits.

Anna

After working in Beijing for two years, the company decided to cease its international downstream operations, and I was told to close the office and repatriate. I was shocked but quickly realized I had to explain to two important constituents why we were changing course and how I could help. First, I had to manage a graceful exit out of the country knowing that, at some point, relationships would be rebuilt when we returned. My team and I visited every partner and prospective partner to explain the company's change in strategy and emphasize that it was not viewed as lack of confidence in China. Second, I took care of my staff. I found employment in Western companies for all my local staff, knowing that they had become accustomed, both personally and professionally, to working for a large multinational company. I found each one of them a job. As I turned off the lights and closed the door, I felt a twinge of sadness for what I would not be able to see through because of no fault of my own.

Although I didn't realize it at the time, Amoco saw this experience as directly relevant to my next job as vice president of the international business unit. In this capacity, I was to extricate our downstream business from several other markets: Eastern Europe, Mexico, and Russia. I had the dubious honor of repeating the last scene of the China experience all over again three more times!

I was determined to learn from the mistakes made by others as I helped to right the wrongs of past short-term strategic decisions and begin to effect long-term change in the way international operations were run at Amoco. For six months, I did the job and learned from it. I learned that strategies needed to be robust and able to withstand short-term discontinuities. Commitment to enter a country needs to be well thought through, with the understanding that immediate wins might not occur. Sitting in a corporate office and making decisions about business in other countries that you fly in and out of is not wise because you cannot glean enough insight to make the right decision. At this point in my career, I realized the importance of being based abroad and living in country to make the best global business decisions. Successfully and diplomatically handling these less-than-ideal situations made me a stronger leader.

I needed this learning under my belt, for in less than two years, I was asked to take on a role in the restructuring of Amoco once the merger with British Petroleum (BP) was announced. I tapped my international connections to advocate for and assign many of the Amoco professionals to international postings. I knew it would be critical to their future development in this much more global company, so I placed people in Spain, Singapore, South Africa, the UK, and Australia. In my first formal assignment, I was named business unit leader for BP/Amoco based in Atlanta, Georgia, where the two companies had parallel organizations. Over the next six months, I had to lay off 40 percent of the staff – one of the most difficult assignments I have ever had to do. Upon completion, I was rewarded with a promotion to a group vice president of emerging markets in London in mid-1999. I drew on my experience in China as we considered developing beachhead businesses in new geographies.

After only eighteen months, I was named global vice president marketing, reporting to the deputy CEO and meeting frequently with the CEO to discuss marketing and the power of branding. I believe I influenced his thinking on the power of reputation and branding. BP launched its "green" campaign, and the positive impact was astounding. I enjoyed this global role but soon came to realize that I would likely continue in

168

this same role at BP for the rest of my career. The company was most likely to continue to be run by engineers who were male and British, with strong upstream backgrounds. I was none of these. Although I had succeeded further and faster than most women in a male-dominated industry and company, I felt as if I would never be named to one of the top seven leadership positions to which I aspired. And so, at the age of forty-three, I left my senior position at BP, packed up with my husband and children, and moved from London to Vero Beach, Florida, where we had a holiday home. I needed time to think and consider my options. If you ever have the chance to take time off, do it to take stock of the many aspects of your life, rather than be lured into the many opportunities that immediately avail themselves to you as a successful professional woman. It was the best decision I ever made.

Chapter 8

Ensuring a Successful Return

After your time abroad, do not take the next job unless you truly believe it will challenge and excite you more than the one you are leaving – unless you have a change in your personal situation and want to pull back on your career for a while. You've earned more than just a decent position, and you probably won't be happy with just a "normal" job. Take time to search out the right position back in your home market or HQ. It will be worth the effort and critical to your professional advancement and personal happiness.

– Stacie, coauthor and consultant

Whether it's after two or ten years abroad, eventually you will probably decide to return to your home market or HQ. Professionally, there are many reasons to return. For many, the agreed-upon term is up, and either the employee or the company wants to end that specific engagement. Sometimes you're offered a position you can't refuse, despite your desire to continue living overseas. You may feel as though you've accomplished as much as you can in this market and want to move on to a bigger job. Perhaps you want experience in another business unit or country or the opportunity to work with a particular leader.

Personally, you may have had enough of living overseas. Your spouse may have decided that he's had enough. You may want to return to be closer to elderly or sick parents, or your children may have educational or personal growth needs that you believe are best met in your home country. Whatever the reason, there are steps you can take to ensure the most successful return possible.

171

More Triumph than Trial

Do not take a job just to take a job. After your stint abroad, you must be challenged, you must be able to exercise your entrepreneurial skills, and you must have some latitude in which to do it – or you probably won't be happy. For the lucky, opportunity knocks, and all they have to do is open the door. The rest of us must pursue a specific position and work to get it. Still others respond and react to a company's first offer, many times a naïve offer by someone in HR who doesn't know any better. If there is one piece of advice we can give you about your return, it's this: do not expect others to know what is best for you. Most likely, they won't.

All the experts agree the most successful repatriations occur when companies work closely with their returning employees who, in turn, do most of the legwork in determining what kinds of roles they want, what new skills they bring to the table, and what type of environment would be ideal. For the past several years, you may have run an office or plant, managed a large team, or served as the most senior person in an overseas location. You have taken risks, created something big out of nothing (or very little), and beat the odds. You need to determine whether you would like a traditional or nontraditional job. Heading up a department, leading a global brand or major client, or overseeing the financials of a large division may *seem* like a promotion to HR, your colleagues, or even you. But you have to be very careful not be duped by the title, the numbers, or the size of team, budget, or sales alone. It's the *experience* that will determine your job satisfaction. The latter could be something new and different – a job in uncharted territory or perhaps the creation of a new position. The nontraditional roles may have a small team and budget, but you may enjoy them more because you can usually operate autonomously. You'll need to look diligently for such roles; they're not always obvious. Treat your return as a challenge in getting the best job possible to meet your specific objectives and desires.

Making It Real

Living abroad felt amazing. Being able to return home with a great job made me feel triumphant!

– **Perry, coauthor and Kraft Foods, Inc.**

My years of working for large American multinational companies in China enabled me to become proficient in Mandarin and to build a network of colleagues and business contacts. Later, when I decided – primarily for personal reasons – to come home to the United States and leave full-time corporate employment, I was able to leverage my experience in China into a consulting business, providing counsel to American companies trying to enter the China market today. All told, I make more money "per hour" than I did in China, and I work about half the number of hours. This is a direct result of my access to regional company presidents and general managers in China, which is a direct consequence of the time I spent living and working overseas.

– Rebecca, consultant

My international background continues to add a certain mark of excellence that my clients value.

– Lisa, VogtGoldstein

I cannot imagine that I would have transitioned from journalist to business management had I stayed in the United States This new job not only brought greater financial rewards but it helped identify me for bigger roles in the business.

– Nancy, Columbia University

Keep an open mind and be flexible. Don't accept the standard ways of doing things as necessarily best for you.

– Anna, former BP executive

After spending four years working in Asia-Pacific and the Middle East, I leveraged the contacts I had made overseas to land a senior-level job in the Bush Administration at the U.S. Agency for International Development (USAID). I entered the government agency as the global head of public affairs responsible for communication in more than a hundred countries. I moved on to become the Agency's first chief branding officer after I developed a brand for U.S foreign assistance to ensure the American people were credited for our aid. It's the most important thing I've ever done. And it would not have been possible if I hadn't had the opportunity to work with the former Secretary of State Colin L. Powell as part of my overseas experience.

– Joanne, USAID

I went to Russia because I knew it would help me get ahead faster: the opportunities to learn, to do more, but more importantly to be recognized for my ability to get things done regardless of the obstacles. I didn't speak Russian, had only read Tolstoy, and had visited the country once, but I wanted to work abroad. I was looking for an adventure. After four and a half years in Russia, I returned to the United States and started my own business. Then a company recruited me into a great job. It was definitely worth it!

— **Pam, Westinghouse**

The most grown-up decision I've ever made was to quit my job as group vice president, marketing at BP and do something I had never done before — not work full time. My time overseas boosted my confidence and gave me a life of infinite possibilities.

— **Anna, former BP executive**

Enhanced Personal and Professional Skills

One critical component to finding the best position is understanding how you have changed and how to make the most of it. The most common changes women have reported are the following:

- **Better communication skills.** Having had to deal with language differences, cultural innuendos, and subtle nuances, you have become a better listener and communicator. You have learned to pay close attention to everything you say, how you say it, and how it is received.

- **Enhanced business acumen.** You have been doing business in another country and have learned new laws, regulations, currencies, and standard operating practices. You have had increased responsibility in managing the financials if you've been in a small office or plant.

- **More robust capabilities.** You have entered new situations, learned new skills, and devised solutions for problems you didn't know existed, all within a different and often challenging environment. Your abilities have been tested, strengthened, and honed.

- **Stronger management skills.** Managing across cultures, across times zones, and then back "home" requires a flexibility not required in most domestic professional situations. You have been managing employees, supervisors, clients, and customers in a totally new environment. You probably have failed in some instances and thus have learned from your mistakes.

- **Enhanced ability to build relationships.** Figuring out who to influence, how to motivate a team, and how to inspire confidence in the people you meet are just a few of the ways you have built relationships with those you need to be successful on the ground. Most women also note the lifelong friendships with other global citizens as an important element of personal growth.

- **Greater acceptance of diversity.** Knowing what it feels like to be a minority and demonstrating empathy and understanding in cross-cultural situations in which you are the one who is foreign increases your appreciation for and tolerance of diversity.

Making It Real

By living in another country's mindset, your perspective changes as you learn how others make decisions, how their perceptions differ, and what makes them tick. When you are a marketer, this knowledge is priceless – and you can't learn it in b-school.

– Lisa, VogtGoldstein

Working overseas teaches you the things you can't learn in school or from books. No matter how much you've heard about it from others, you must experience it yourself to know what we mean. My time spent with one company in New York enabled me to advance my career significantly with another company back in Hong Kong.

– Lisa, Hong Kong Baptist University

My greatest growth took place in management, specifically because of the amount I learned about myself. I failed a few times but picked myself up and moved on stronger and better than before. It wasn't easy, but recognizing why I failed led directly to future successes.

– Stacie, coauthor and consultant

Living overseas enriched my life. It made a difference professionally, yes; but for me, the learning was much more about personal growth. My time abroad gave me the possibility to meet special people who continue to have a positive impact on my life, still today.

– Eleonora, Twilight Music

Working overseas is the ultimate diversity experience.

– Donna, former U.S. Ambassador to Brazil, Venezuela, Bolivia, and the Dominican Republic

Just Another Day at the Office

Once you've found the right job for you, it's time to get back to work. You may expect a big welcome because while overseas you've achieved things that have proved your value to the company beyond doubt. However, your colleagues, your supervisor, and even HR (who is supposed to know better) may not know how to accord you proper respect. Help them. First, be humble. Be willing to admit that you need their help because you have been away for a while. Second, quantify your learnings for your own and the company's use. You've probably already done this in the packaging and marketing you've done to land this new job, but your new team members and coworkers may not know. Sharing this insight will help your colleagues, customers, and clients better understand what international employees learn and bring back. Third, reconnect with old and new colleagues alike. Pretend you're a new employee and ask people to lunch, ask for help on certain projects, and get to know your office neighbors. Be part of the home team. Do not dwell on the details of your overseas experience. If people express an interest in learning more, perhaps you can offer to do a brown-bag lunch presentation. This will seem less like bragging and more like sharing. Fourth, work hard. Don't expect things to come easily. You are new to this office; you must build your network, and learn the ropes again. You may be a little rusty in things local, as they may have changed while you were gone.

Preparing Yourself

Many returning individuals find that they suffer from reverse culture shock when they return home. You expect things to be as they were when you left, but they aren't. You have to grow accustomed to dealing with this new environment. It's not too dissimilar from when you first moved abroad: the same skills and approach apply. You can do it, and you will.

176

But it takes time. Most returning professionals experience the same basic symptoms of malaise and disorientation. These are listed below, along with tried-and-true advice on how to combat them.

- **You are just one of many.** In most overseas offices, the foreigner stands out. You are different culturally, if not also in appearance, and you probably had a prestigious role. But once you return – especially if it's back to HQ – you will be just like the others. What to do? Accept it, and work to differentiate yourself in new ways. Jump into your new role with energy and dedication, and do not expect to be treated differently. If you have taken the right position, you will soon shine again. Be *patient but persistent*.

- **You miss the excitement, the buzz, the intensity of living abroad**. The challenging, stimulating, exciting, even gut-wrenching moments of working abroad make you feel more alive. Your "old life" may be more predictable and comfortable, but it will probably lack the added spice of living in a foreign land. What to do? Stay in close contact with your international network, including other returnees. Add new things to your life, such as those inspired by or continued from your posting. Begin to *build new relationships*.

- **You have less autonomy and more rules to follow.** You have grown used to operating without a net. You have made decisions fast, often with little or no support. Once you return to mainstream operations, there are many more bureaucratic hoops to jump through, and people's buy-ins to secure. That makes the process of problem-solving more cumbersome and frustrating. What to do? Accept the hierarchy and follow the rules or diplomatically suggest ways to improve them. Demonstrate your initiative and entrepreneurial abilities, and get yourself noticed in small ways at first before expanding. Your own initiative is critical to keeping your career on the fast track. Stay *flexible*, following the bends in the road.

- **You are not the same person as you reenter this environment.** Your relationships with friends, neighbors, co-workers, and family will seem different – and they will be different – because you've changed. You've seen the world and broadened your horizons beyond your hometown. What to do? Accept who you are. Make new friends

177

and keep in touch with the old. Explore your surroundings. Be a tourist in your own land. Be *curious and open* to your new surroundings.

- **Other people are not interested in your experiences.** It will be a big shock when you realize that people really aren't interested in where you've been and what you've done. It's not just out of jealousy or malice, although that could be part of it. They simply can't relate to your adventure. Your stories, your insights, even your jokes cannot generally be appreciated by someone who hasn't been in a similar situation. Your colleagues and friends will prefer to talk about the weather, local sports franchises, or even someone's garden down the street. What to do? Express an interest in them. Do not come across as a bore; learn to speak about your overseas experiences for short bits of time and only when the situation warrants. Use your experiences to add value and help solve problems, but do not make it obvious. Be the *good listener and communicator* that you are.

Those same traits that made you successful overseas will ensure your success in your return as well. Don't forget what you learned or think it doesn't apply now that you're home. It does! Your continued success is just as important as your success abroad. Prove that you can do both!

You will experience ups and downs. Ride them out. Stay connected to your network. If you persist, you will prevail. Your colleagues will learn to accept and appreciate your difference, company leaders will appreciate the investment they made and the value you bring through advancement, and you will continue to move upward. If you feel that you are not moving ahead – and companies often change or restructure, and you may end up with a different job or a boss who does not know of or appreciate your international skills – keep your options option. Although companies are improving the way they handle returnees – some employees do end up unhappy and leave. That's unfortunate for the company, but it usually turns out well for the employee. Executive search firms confirm that returning expats top their lists as some of the best employees to place. But try to make it work with your employer – you owe it to each other.

As we wrap up our journey, let's see how our six women used the experience and wisdom gained overseas to open up a world of opportunities at home.

The Journey Continues

Stacie

My husband and I decided that it was time to return to the United States. His mother and stepfather were pushing eighty, and the health of one was beginning to fail. Although Burson-Marsteller wanted me to continue in Hong Kong, they accepted my decision to return to Washington, D.C. I fulfilled my three-year commitment overseas and returned to the same office with a significant promotion – but after taking a four-month unpaid sabbatical. We traveled throughout Asia, planning an itinerary that took us back to some of our favorite spots, such as Vietnam, and a few new ones like Laos, Cambodia, Burma, and southern India. Our travels were amazing, and as we sat on the runway at the new Hong Kong International airport (Kai Tak, the one famous for its 90-degree banked turns in between the apartment buildings of Kowloon, closed during our time there), I thought how much had changed – the airport, the government, the economic stability, myself, my new marriage. I admit to getting a little weepy, but it was also hard to not smile, thinking of the great progress made and the future ahead.

Before I even stepped foot into the office or bought a house or a car, I found out I was pregnant – with twins! This sooner-than-planned event did not affect my rapid promotion to managing director. Owing to my good working relationships with senior clients back in Asia, I landed a senior role on B-M's largest client and for an agency person, having a client to work on the day you set foot back into your home office is a very important thing. If you don't have any clients, you are perceived as overhead – not a good thing for someone just returning to an office filled with ambitious, smart go-getters.

During this time, I took six months off to give birth to my twin daughters and returned to work telecommuting most days (an uncommon arrangement at the time, but one I was able to negotiate because of my track record) and commuting to New York City from Washington, D.C., another two days. Within two years of my return, at the age of thirty-four, I was leading B-M's fourth-highest revenue generator. I was named a WPP (Burson-Marsteller's parent company) partner, top 1 percent of a 65,000-strong company of agencies, one of the top 25 professionals at the world's most successful PR firm, and considered as a future contender for a top management job. I would not have been given such tremendous opportunities with only ten years of experience had I not proved myself time and again while working in Asia and then leading a global client upon my return.

As a senior client leader of a global client, I traveled a great deal. I found it difficult, as many women do, to balance work and home life. Feeling very confident in what I had achieved thus far and a strong urge to take a break and enjoy my children led me to switch to an in-house position at Unilever. I did so for two years, reorganizing, rebuilding, and leading the North American corporate affairs team. I was responsible for advising senior management on internal and external positioning, including the consolidation of multiple business units into one $11 billion operating company and the launch of the company's new corporate brand. But I didn't enjoy it as much as the meritocracy I had left. And so I left Unilever in 2005: started my own consulting business, including working with the Jane Goodall Institute; and decided to reassess my options. I've been busy writing and promoting this book, while I work on getting a few other book ideas into the pipeline. I absolutely love the freedom I have using my international experience and network to share knowledge and information with other women. Every now and then I feel the pull of the glamour and glory of being a senior leader in a multinational ... but, for now, I'm fulfilled. Next year, who knows.

Diane

I got a call from my boss saying that the CEO was coming to visit and that we needed to clean up the place, get everybody prepped, and write a thirty-page presentation to showcase the plant's progress. Without having enough time to go home, I had to ask my husband, Ed, to bring me a suit and pumps so I'd look presentable! It all went well, and a few weeks later I got a call from an old boss wondering if I'd like to be special assistant to the CEO. I resisted at first. Why would I want to leave a job that I had struggled with yet become successful in? I had autonomy, was running a 350-person plant, and was making money for the company. I loved living in Europe. I was torn, and I didn't want to leave, but I knew it was an opportunity I shouldn't pass up. This was my chance to do strategic planning, work on projects that were coming down the pipeline, and be involved in making decisions about the future of the company. I took it and went back to Wilmington.

Our move went reasonably smoothly because Ed and I moved back into the same house we left, and I went to work on the same campus. We had friends and family nearby and settled back in, albeit wistful every now and then for a weekend in the Alps or the South of France!

On one hand my return was easier than most expats because I went straight into a high-profile role. I worked with the CEO almost every day, and I attended all board meetings and all strategy and planning sessions within the various business units. I worked with the top one hundred leaders in the company and was able to cement my network internally and externally – even after spending five years overseas. On the other hand, there was no room for failure. The job was high-risk and high-reward. I was "on" working for the CEO twelve hours a day. There was a fifty-fifty chance of failure, and you can be sure I had very sweaty palms. I emerged successfully, having developed my own philosophies of leadership. I had been exposed to good and bad leaders and their relevant traits and styles. The time I spent working with the CEO was incredible. Eighteen months later, I was ready to move on. I picked the leader I would learn the most from, taking on the title of director of business development for nylon fibers. It was a global position, and after another eighteen months, I was promoted again.

My career continued to progress, and I now serve as a member of DuPont's executive management team. I run the largest DuPont business unit – a $7-billion operation with a 7,500-strong global team. I believe that I am significantly better as a global manager because of the time I spent working overseas. Being a woman has made a significant difference in my success as well. Throughout my career, I leveraged my traits as a woman, such as being more sensitive – not just "here to help you" – but figuring out the best way to help, engender support, and enable teams to do well under my leadership, and then beyond, after I left.

Anna

Repatriation was hell! My kids did not understand why I was quitting and why we were moving, especially when I was taking them away from a lifestyle they had come to love for five years. They attended the American School in London, had grown accustomed to having friends around the world, and enjoyed the expat lifestyle of Alpine ski trips over long weekends, Easters in Italy, and winter vacations in Thailand. That kind of excitement and variety is tough to give up. We moved to Sugar Land, Texas, where my elderly parents as well as my youngest sister and her family lived.

During this time I interviewed with many companies that could only offer me more of what I had left at BP. I decided that I didn't want to do it all over again and wondered in what other ways I could leverage my experience. I enjoyed the board I sat on and realized that my marketing savvy and global experience could be leveraged into many industries. I also knew that I wanted to spend more time with my family: kids, husband, and parents. I chose to build a diverse board portfolio, I have joined three thus far, and enjoy it immensely. The boards on which I serve value my experience and provide me with the challenge, diversity, and flexibility that I want at this stage in my life. I have not looked back once at my decision, nor do I miss the daily grind of executive life!

While I consider whether I continue to only serve on boards, follow my entrepreneurial muse, or become the CEO or president of a major corporation, I marvel at the options in front of me – options that I created for myself through years of hard work, perseverance, and, yes, my time abroad. Living overseas truly changed me, my husband, and my children for the better. Our worlds have expanded. I have learned many things that broadened my personal and professional horizons, made my life richer, and increased my cultural awareness. It boosted my confidence and inspired me to take risks that I wouldn't otherwise have taken. Above all, succeeding as a woman added one more element to the mix of my experience and gave me something that many men didn't have. The global playing field was in many ways more level than the field domestically. I have every confidence this will continue to be the case for women today and in the future.

Patricia

I knew it was time to start laying the groundwork to leave Russia by mid-1998. By then I had been there a total of six years and had accomplished most of my goals. I was working for a prestigious publication, I had a clip book full of stories, I had saved a lot of money, and I had lived through some dramatic events. Nothing seemed new to me anymore – the kiss of death for a journalist. If you're not excited about a story, you can be sure the reader won't be either (to say nothing of your editor). Then came the last straw. The Russian government defaulted on its debt and devalued the ruble, sending the economy into a crisis and many businesses into bankruptcy, including those of some of my friends. Once again, the Russians were confirming the beliefs of their many critics – that they couldn't be trusted, that the rule of law would never take hold. I was disillusioned.

I talked to my editors back home and asked to be transferred out within a year, thus giving myself plenty of time to find a position outside Russia. One editor offered Germany, but I knew it would seem too sedate after the chaos of Russia. I also wanted to be closer to my parents, who were getting on in years. I agreed to move to New York and switch from being a reporter/writer to being an editor, something I had never really wanted to be. I loved being out and about and getting information firsthand from movers and shakers and the man on the street. Most of all, I loved generating ideas and being the first one to write about something. But the editor-in-chief persuaded me. So I packed up and moved to New York as Europe editor in 1999. Within a year I was promoted to editor of the entire European edition. In that role I edited stories, including covers. I also worked with the reporters, deciding which stories they would pursue, and with photo and art directors, choosing the pictures, illustrations, and graphics for each story. I worked closely with the top editors to determine which stories would run each week.

After five years in the same job, I got restless again in 2005. In confidence, I told one of the assistant managing editors that I was ready for a change. He knew and liked my work and told me that internal changes were coming. He offered to mention my name whenever an interesting position came up. I didn't have to wait very long. In a few months, the new editor-in-chief and new executive editor asked me if I would like to fill a newly created position of national news editor. They believed that I could handle deadline pressures and work collegially with a lot of the heavy-hitters on the staff. I took the job, and thank goodness I did. One month later, in a cost-cutting move, the editor-in-chief announced we were closing *BusinessWeek*'s European and Asian editions and putting the global stories online instead.

Putting out a weekly magazine is a group effort that takes a lot of compromise, tact, flexibility, and attention to detail – skills I developed in Russia. If I hadn't had the courage to go way back then, I wouldn't be where I am today. In June 2007 I accepted a job at the *New York Times* as deputy editor of the Sunday business section. There I will be editing big feature and investigative stories. I know my experience in Moscow helped me get the job because it proved I have grit, patience, and wide-ranging curiosity. While most of the stories will be focused on American companies and people, I will be able to work with foreign correspondents on international stories as well. The world, especially the world of business, is increasingly global. Overseas experience is a valuable asset.

Perry

For the communications industry, New York is the ultimate proving ground. So after nearly ten years abroad, I decided it was time to return to the United States. My employer was very willing to help me find the right spot, since I had delivered for them in every role I'd held. However, there really wasn't a bigger and better opening that I wanted. Once you've counseled global CEOs, toured with former heads of state, run an office in Russia, and helped educate hundreds of millions ex-communists about privatization, being "just another managing director" isn't that appealing. I needed to do something different to make my return interesting and challenging enough. Luckily, a recent client from Unilever Latin America had just been promoted to the top post in North America. He asked if I would be interested in becoming a vice president of corporate affairs for Unilever North America – thus proving my belief that you need to network and always do the best job you can because you never know where your former clients, colleagues, friends, or foes are going to end up!

Although I hadn't worked in the United States for years, he was confident I could do the job, and he wanted an American with international experience because Unilever was a European company. So in 2000, I moved to the New York area. It turned out to be another smart career risk and a great four years. I honed my corporate affairs skills, but even more importantly, I learned about corporate life and got a "hands-on MBA" from the many smart folks who were willing to teach me about everything from supply chains to innovation funnels to balance sheets. Then, during a major restructuring in 2004, a new head of North America was brought in and my position and most of the department was eliminated, I was eight months pregnant at the time and was convinced that it was the worst thing that could possibly happen. But, as it turns out, it was one of the best. Unilever was very generous regarding severance, and I took six months off to enjoy my little miracle. After that, I wanted to go back to work but didn't want another big corporate job – at least not yet. So I taught at a local university, set up my own consulting business, joined the national board of the Girl Scouts of the USA, and started writing this book. Just as I was settling into my new life, Kraft came knocking. Since I'd spent most of my career abroad and hadn't applied for a job in more than fifteen years, I didn't know many head hunters in the United States. But this headhunter found me through two old friends with whom I'd worked in London. Kraft liked the breadth and depth of my corporate affairs expertise and my knowledge of the consumer products industry. But what really set me apart from their other candidates was my global experience. My family agreed that the opportunity was worth going for, so we moved from Westport, Connecticut, the town we'd grown to love, to Chicago. It wasn't an easy move. It was my first move with a family – something far more complex than just moving yourself. Plus, my expectations were off base. Sometimes it's harder to move "nearby" than it is to move around the world. When you go to Bangkok, you expect it to be different. I didn't fully appreciate the differences between the East Coast and the Midwest. Now that we are into our second year, things are feeling better, and all the positives I'd counted on are shining through the gray days, especially this region's emphasis on family. As for my career at Kraft, that has progressed well. Just fourteen months after joining the company, at the age of forty-two, I was promoted from vice president to senior vice president and head of international corporate affairs, a role I really enjoy — one I never would have gotten if I hadn't taken that leap of faith and headed for Singapore seventeen years ago.

Jackie

Throughout my one year at Swissair, I learned all kinds of things about myself and others. I was placed in a totally unfamiliar environment and high-stress situation. I had to use every fiber of technical knowledge I had, learn a few new things on the fly, and operate within the confines of a legal jurisdiction with which I was not familiar — all the while managing a crisis within an industry that is center stage. Politics, the media, and emotions have a tremendous impact on the airline industry, and numerous stakeholders have to be managed. Once 9/11 happened, we knew the odds were against us. On October 1, 2001, Swissair officially announced its intention to file for bankruptcy under Swiss bankruptcy laws. The filing was accepted by the courts a few days later, and the process that would see the Swissair Group dismantled as a conglomerate company began.

After it was over, my phone started ringing off the wall with all kinds of companies interested in helping me help them through a bankruptcy, crisis, or some other extremely difficult circumstance. I considered many offers. I knew that my next move would have to be both challenging and exciting.

I had stayed in touch with Nestle, and to the credit of the people there, they knew what I might be looking for and why. As it turned out, Nestle was going to take Alcon public, and it offered me the CFO role. My experience as the CFO of a publicly listed company, combined with my knowledge of the American stock market, Alcon, and Nestle, made it a natural. I would be able to keep the parent company happy while doing the best on-the-ground job for Alcon. I would be managing multiple stakeholders in the United States and Switzerland. I weighed this offer against all the others received, and I accepted. With great success, we took Alcon public in 2002.

Once again I found myself in a new industry; I had worked for the past six years outside of Alcon, and the ophthalmic industry had changed quite a bit. I used this lack of knowledge to create a comfortable environment in which to return. I left Alcon's Texas operations nine years before as a midlevel finance person. I returned as the CFO. I had to use the right mixture of diplomacy, humility, and patience to rebuild relationships with the Alcon team. I spent a lot of time thinking about how I interacted with others, and it paid off. My lack of up-to-date knowledge of the industry made me dependent on others who knew more. As I learned, I was able to demonstrate my skill set and demonstrate the value my global experience brought to the table. Returning expats have a tough time of it after being gone almost ten years – especially if it's the United States. So much has changed that it takes some getting used to, especially after you've emerged from achieving great stuff. Humility is a good thing.

After being back now for more than four years, I can say there are things I miss. I'm lucky to be back near my family, but I miss the international lifestyle and diversity of people found in other countries and international cities. As for what's next for me, I suppose I would say that the sky's the limit, to some extent. The Alcon opportunity, for which I am very grateful, has given me the added experience of taking a company public, successfully dealing with the early years of Sarbanes-Oxley and a changing corporate governance environment, satisfying independent shareholders and a majority shareholder simultaneously, and managing through significant changes in the ophthalmic segment of the healthcare industry. So what's next? Let's just say that I'll be on the lookout for the next challenge and the next opportunity to stretch myself even further. If you leave yourself open to opportunity, you never know where you might end up.

Conclusion

Now that our journey together has come full circle, we hope our tales have excited your imagination and ignited your adventurous spirit to explore a whole new world of opportunities. Going global can fast-track your career and expand your horizons both personally and professionally in ways you might not have considered before.

We trust that now you're better prepared to take off on your own adventure in the international marketplace. Understanding the global arena is critical to businesses today, and the same is true for anyone who wants to get ahead. We hope what you've learned here will help you choose the best market and identify the most strategic opportunity to ensure your success above and beyond your and your company's expectations. Your overseas achievements will enhance your reputation and set you apart from your peers. This elevated profile then provides a platform from which to promote your accomplishments, which you must do to ensure recognition and advancement.

It won't be easy. You will have good days and bad days. You will be stretched, strained, and constantly challenged. But you will also have fun – probably the time of your life.

So, get ahead by going abroad. It worked for us, and it can for you, too. If you want it, go for it. Start your journey today.